Rock Springs Review

Anthology ~ 2017

Judy Stock
Editor

This is primarily a work of fiction. Most characters, places, and incidents are the product of the authors' imaginations or are used fictitiously. Any resemblance to actual persons, living or dead, is entirely coincidental. Statements or opinions expressed in the stories and articles of this publications are those of the authors and do not necessarily represent the views or opinions of any person or entity associated with the publication of this book.

Rock Springs Review
Anthology ~ 2017

ISBN-10: 978-0-9895069-3-9

Cover Photo: The Write Place © 2016
              Marilyn Hope Lake, Ph.D.

Printed in the United States of America

Dedication

In memory of my writer friend, Anita Crews, who always loved to try something new.

The last thing she did with her writing was to take on the challenge of writing a sestina. She wrote several of them, and said it never became any easier. She was about as stubborn as I am, so she just kept writing.

Her final sestina went through several iterations.

I was too close to the poet to be objective about the end product, but to honor her, I have included it in this anthology.

God bless you, Anita. You are resting in His love.

಼ ಼

Acknowledgements

A special thank you, all of you authors who have entrusted your "children" to my editorial and publishing skills. I hope I have lived up to your expectations.

Thank you for your patience. This year has been "a long road," and many of the miles weren't paved.

Thank you, Dr. Marilyn Hope Lake, for the cover photograph of a favorite writing place of yours.

("The Write Place" is one of her photographs in the *Ekphrastic Writing Workbook, Volume I*, a collaboration between Dr. Lake and Denton Warn.)

Thank you, members of Boonslick Creative Writers who allowed me to add your interpretations of one of the prompts used at a group meeting. I think all of us said, "Wow!" at that meeting.

A special, upfront thank you readers. Where on earth would we be without you? If you like our Rock Springs Review Anthology 2017, how about going on Amazon and writing a review.

૨ ૭

Foreword

Daren Dean, instructor at Louisiana State University and author of the nationally known novel, *Beyond the Pale,* began the *Rock Springs Review* while a student at the University of Missouri-Columbia. The premiere issue was published in 1996. Dean's goal was to provide access for mid-western students and new writers to a quality literary journal. Daren Dean is proud that Judy Stock, who took over the journal in 1998, has continued the mission.

From the Judge's Picks in poetry, fiction and nonfiction through Other Contributions, the pieces in this anthology enlighten, touch our emotions, and make us smile. They delve into love and life, life and death, grieving and grievances.

Comprised of lyrical poetry, diverse and well-honed prose, and accurate historical pieces, *Rock Springs Review, Anthology ~ 2017* is an outstanding addition to literary collections.

As both writers and readers, we thank Judy Stock for using her years of experience as an editor to produce this wonderful new anthology.

Marilyn Hope Lake, Ph.D.
November 2017

ঙ ঙ

Preface

I love anthologies, simply because they are such fun. Several authors write several prose or poetry pieces from several inspirations. The final effect is a collection of intriguing reading.

The reader can leaf through the book partaking of a poem here, an essay there, and a short story somewhere else.

Sometimes anthologies have a theme. A themed anthology allows the reader to see how the authors observe, interpret, and write to a particular topic.

Other anthologies, like this one, show authors writing their own things. A poem or story can make you wonder where in the universe the writer came up with such an idea.

This anthology started out as a contest. I remain amazed by the writing talent available. The winning entries are at the beginning of the book.

Who knows what next year may bring. Maybe we will do this again, or maybe we will do something different.

> Judy Stock
> Editor/Publisher
> Rock Springs Review

ॐ ॐ

Table of Contents

Judges

Judges' Picks: Poetry

Judges' Picks: Fiction

Judges' Picks: Nonfiction

Other Contributions

ଛ ଶ

Contest
Winners

Judges

Fiction: Susan Satterfield

Susan Satterfield is the author of a number of published short stories and poems including "The Lady Killer" and "Sweet Teddy" which appeared in an anthology entitled *Small Bites*. Her Yard Dog stories include "What Goes Around" *(Flush Fiction) and* "A Bad Case of the Munchies" (*I Should Have Stayed in Oz)*. Her poem entitled "The Hunger: A Zombie Poem" was published by Costcom. Her latest sale is entitled "Stranded at the Gates of Hell," which is in the anthology *Flush Fiction II* from Yard Dog Press.

Currently, Susan teaches online, hybrid, and traditional courses including composition, creative writing, and Introduction to Literature at MCC-Longview Community College. She lives in Lee's Summit, Missouri, with her family including dogs and an ornery black cat.

NonFiction: Donna Volkenannt

Donna Volkenannt was born in the Midwest and has lived in the Southwest, the Northwest, and in Europe, but reading and writing have taken her imagination to countless other faraway places. First place winner of the University of Dayton's 2012 Erma Bombeck Global Humor award, and top-ten finalist in the 2014 Global

Human Interest category, she lives in St. Peters with her husband, their grandchildren, and one loveable black Lab.
http://donnasbookpub.blogspot.com

Poetry: Larry Allen

Larry W. Allen has had poems published in *Main Street Rag*, *The Hatchet*, *Mid-America Poetry Review*, *Boston Literary Magazine*, *Fine Arts Discovery*, and other publications. His book, *Do Come In And Other Lizzie Borden Poems* was published by Pear Tree Press. Larry is a retired probation officer who lives in Columbia, Missouri.

ᛒ ᛪ

Judges' Picks:

℘~℘

Poetry

Mary Silwance
1st Place

Arabic

Speak to me
   in a language
    I understand
let your words flow
    like water washing lentils
incense infused with garlic
   punctuate your meaning
with the clamor of Cairo's traffic
     bring your tidings
like onion merchants at dawn,
     basal l'il bey
the Qur'an at dusk
    Allahu 'akbar
and cooing pigeons
   that brood
on my grandmother's
    sand-laced veranda.

ଘ ଵ

Billie Holladay Skelley

2nd Place

Tea for Two

I've often wondered how
the conversation might flow
if two poets, like Emily and Sylvia,
could slip the bonds of death
and cross the miles of time
to visit together
over a steaming cup of hot Earl Grey.
The invitation might read:
"Miss Dickinson, please join Miss Plath for tea
at the Poets' Corner Café today at half past three."
These two wordsmiths might speak freely
about truth, beauty, and fidelity—
and converse without a care—
but their thoughts might also
turn sharply
to loneliness, loss, and
the depths of despair.
After a few sips of their fortifying brews,
would they dare wade into the waters
of heartbreak
and the sorrow that ensues?
Or would the topic of death
be the special on this afternoon's menu?
Perhaps they'd both regard
death,
as a warm cloak to wear,
a comforting form of release
from all their earthly cares.

Just maybe, they'd agree
their feelings are not so rare.
Perhaps these two women
would simply sit in silence,
and allow no words to pass
their lips.
They might gaze longingly
into one another's
eyes
seeking a sisterly soul
to recognize.
Sipping their tea silently,
they might just
realize
that kindred spirits
need no words to
empathize.

Mary Silwance
3rd Place

Ledger

Virginia Woolf
walked into a river,
pockets full of rocks.

How did she know she had enough

to counterbalance madness
or
enough madness to require rocks?

Did she weigh each against her pain,
a ledger of suffering?

If she had, instead, lined them up
one by speckled one, there
on the snarling shore,
relieving the strained fabric of her sweater

could tears and time
dissolve their dense weight?

Enough

to free her

from death
into breath

Judges' Picks:

୫୦ ~ ୦ଓ

Fiction

Jane Hale

1st Place

A Rose

He came to my florist shop, Bloomers, every Friday just about closing time. He always wore work clothes and a smile. He always bought the same thing, a rose.

One rainy Friday our clock chimed five p.m. just as the door opened.

Viola, one of our regular customers, was close to tears. "I need some flowers for Mom."

"We close at five." Cindy, my helper, eyed the front window. Outside her boyfriend sat in his truck at the curb.

"You go ahead, Cindy. I'll take care of the customer."

"Oh, I'll be glad to stay," She offered, halfheartedly.

I moved to take her place. "Viola, how are you? The truck delivered your mom's favorite peonies. Would you like—." My attention was drawn to the front door of the shop.

"Sorry, sir, we close at 5:00 pm." Cindy hurried out the door closing it in a customer's face.

"Excuse me, Viola." I hurried to the door, opened it, and saw my Friday evening Rose man starting to walk away.

"Sir! Sir!" I called.

A smile lit up his face. "I thought you were closed."

"I have another customer. Feel free to look around while I finish with her."

Cindy's boyfriend gunned his motor and they pulled away.

"I think some attitude adjustment is needed," I muttered.

He held the door open for me. "You first, Miss...."

"Ginger." I introduced myself.

That afternoon, I got acquainted with Victor Dueck.

Victor talked about his wife, Mary. "She's the brightest flower in my life." As he talked, Victor appeared ten years younger than the forty-five years, he claimed to be. "Mary and I were high school sweethearts. We got married before we were twenty. Her parents were against our marriage. They claimed it would never last. And, here we are, twenty-five years later, still as much in love as we were the day we married."

I admit I was jealous. This was the way I always dreamed a man would love me. "How romantic, Victor. I knew someone special was receiving the rose you take with you every Friday."

The mention of the rose brought Victor back to reality as the clock chimed six. "Sorry, Miss Ginger, you were so kind to keep your shop open so I could get —."

We spoke the words together. "A rose!"

I pulled the rose from the nearby counter where it was wrapped in a green sleeve waiting for him.

Victor held the rose as tenderly as I imagined he might hold Mary.

"Thanks again, Miss Ginger. See you —."

"Next Friday." We chorused.

Victor continued to stop each Friday and purchase Mary a rose.

Each week we continued our conversations.

"Mary and I never had children. Business was good. We bought our dream home several years ago." Victor's life unfolded like the romance novels I read constantly.

"*Bloomers* is my life," I confessed. "I've always loved flowers. My dad died early. Mom and I started *Bloomers* after I graduated college. She died two years ago.

"Life happens. For every flower there is a time and season."

One Friday evening Victor came early. He was restless.

"Is something wrong, Victor?" The thought of him growing tired of our Friday visits panicked me.

"Tomorrow is Mary's birthday. I'm at a loss to know what to get."

"Let's go on a treasure hunt, Victor," I suggested. We visited the department store up the block.

An hour later, our shopping cart held an array of gifts. We moved to the birthday card isle. We read, laughed, and sang along with the musical cards.

Back at *Bloomers*, I offered a bouquet of red roses.

Victor removed a rose. "Consistency, Ginger, is the spice of life."

The next Friday Victor didn't visit *Bloomers*.

I was heartsick. We had a flurry of funeral flowers. I checked the obituary for the correct spelling of a name.

A familiar name leaped out at me. Mary Dueck, wife of Victor Dueck, passed away Monday, September 14, 2016.

Funeral services at the First Baptist Church in Branson at 2:00 pm.

Victor was a true friend. The First Baptist Church was across town. If I caught a cab I could just make the service. I grabbed a single red rose in a green sleeve.

At the church Mary Dueck's service was about to begin but it was private.

"Excuse me, sir?" I asked the funeral director. "Would you give this to Mister Victor Dueck for his wife, Mary?" I handed him the single red rose.

Weeks passed. Victor didn't come to *Bloomers*.

One Friday in December, Cindy said, "Ms. Ginger. A man phoned to see if we delivered flowers to the cemetery."

"What did you tell him?"

She brightened. "We aim to please, right?" She'd never forgotten the attitude adjustments over the years.

"What was the order and where?"

"Evergreen Road, but he only wanted a single, red rose."

I grabbed a red rose. I pulled in the cemetery but realized I didn't know who got the flower.

My cell phone rang. "I bet you're wondering who gets the flower, right?" Cindy asked.

"Yes."

"Turn down the second road. You'll come to a tombstone with a decorative urn. The name on the tombstone is Mary Dueck."

OMG! I was delivering a rose for Victor's wife. The stone read Mary Rose Dueck, beloved wife of Victor Dueck.

"Mary Rose! RIP." I felt a deep kinship with Mary Rose.

Every Friday, I made the trip to Evergreen Cemetery. I placed a fresh rose in the vase beside the Urn. The old rose was always gone.

One Friday, in April the following year, about closing time, I turned to see Victor. He held a box like the one he used to bring Ginger cookies in.

"Hello, Ginger, could we talk over coffee?" Victor looked tired.

Victor had come back! I poured the coffee and helped myself to one of his cookies. Yes, they were homemade, still.

"I have a confession to make, Ginger. My wife is dead." He smiled. "But you know that. Thank you for the weekly roses."

I nodded.

Victor settled in his chair. "Mary Rose bloomed early. We were so in love when we married. She was pregnant before the second year. We were so excited. She believed her parents would come around when the child was born. Then, her parents were killed in a car wreck. Mary Rose's water broke. I rushed her to the hospital. The baby was born dead. No one could explain it but Mary Rose was brain dead, too."

"Oh, Victor." I placed my hand over his.

"I thought my life was over." Victor smiled sadly. "This shadow of a woman wasn't Mary Rose, but she was my responsibility. So, I worked hard to give us a good life. Every Friday I brought her a rose. I told myself she brightened when I gave her the rose, but in my heart, I knew different."

He withdrew his hand and took a sip of coffee. "One day I came to *Bloomers*. I met you, Ginger. It was like I was young again. You were the flower that was blooming in my life. Then, I'd take the rose to Mary. I felt guilty but I kept coming to *Bloomers*. You were like a drug to which I became addicted. So, I baked you cookies and drank coffee with you."

Tears were streaming down my face. I had thought Mary Rose was a healthy, loving, wife. I had coveted the love Victor had for his wife.

"Mary Rose began to get better. Her birthday was coming. I told myself everything might be okay.

"Before I left for work that morning Mary Rose spoke two words. 'Be happy.'

"That night I came to *Bloomers*. We shopped for her birthday. It was one of the happiest days of my life. I took her gifts home expecting her to be happy. But Mary Rose had taken a turn for the worse. She was admitted to the hospital. She died the following week." He began to sob. "All the roses in the world could not bring Mary back. And, all I could think of was you, Ginger." He reached out to touch my hand.

I let my fingers curl around his. I tried to absorb his pain.

"Give me some time, Ginger. Maybe we'll find our time and season."

I gave his hand a reassuring squeeze. "Victor, we've got all the time in the world."

Every Friday, Victor comes by *Bloomers*. We talk, drink coffee, and eat his homemade cookies. Our friendship continues to grow. Feelings of guilt drop away for something we have no need to feel guilt.

A fresh rose continues to be placed in Mary Rose's vase each Friday.

Sometimes when I grow impatient, I remember what Victor said to me one time. "Consistency, Ginger, is the spice of life."

Next Saturday, there's a Flower Convention in the city. I asked Victor to attend. He agreed. Maybe, it's time for our garden to bloom.

ༀ ༀ

Billie Holladay Skelley

2nd Place

Monster Slayers

"Mother, why can't I see Helen?"

"Helen is sick, Judy."

In 1952, one of the worst epidemics in the history of the United States occurred. That year a monster virus stalked the country. It inflicted a disease called poliomyelitis, which often was called simply *polio*. Nearly 58,000 people fought the demon that year. Over 21,000 came away with some degree of paralysis, and more than 3,000 lost their fight.

"Does Helen have the same sickness that killed Daddy?"

"Yes, Judy. Your sister has polio."

"Is Helen going to die, too?"

"I don't know."

The polio virus spread fear. Since healthy children and active adults could be stricken, there appeared to be no rhyme or reason to this fiend. Anyone anywhere could be affected. Previous remedies did not work. Because it struck so indiscriminately, and no one knew how to stop it, polio was terrifying.

"Mother, I'm scared."

"I'm scared, too, Judy."

Eventually, a campaign arose across the country to find a weapon to defeat this scourge. It was called the March of Dimes. For the first time, people felt there was something positive they could do to contribute to the polio monster's demise.

"Should I save my dimes?"

"Yes, Judy. Save them all."

Judy put her dimes in a canister on their local drugstore's counter. On every visit, she stared at the cardboard cutout attached to the container. It featured a girl with crutches and braces on her legs. She looked like Helen, but Judy knew it was not Helen. Her sister, Helen, had died.

"Your dimes," Judy's mother said, "will be used to create a vaccine."

Judy didn't know exactly what a vaccine was, but she knew it was something to stop the polio monster.

Fortunately, the world had two monster slayers: Dr. Jonas Salk and Dr. Albert Sabin. By the mid-1950s and early 1960s, their vaccines were proving effective. The battle against polio began to turn.

On May 27, 1962, Judy's mother woke her before sunrise.

"Put on your best dress, Judy."

"Should I wear my black patent Buster Brown shoes?"

"Yes, but hurry."

Hand in hand, mother and daughter walked to the local elementary school just as the sun was coming up. The doors were locked, but they waited. They stood there for what seemed like hours. A long line formed behind them. Holding her daughter's hand tightly, Judy's mother resolutely waited at the front of the line.

At last, the doors opened.

Maintaining her vise-like grip on her daughter's hand,

Judy's mother walked toward a table where a nurse was sitting. The nurse asked many questions.

"The child's father?"

"Deceased. Polio," Judy's mother answered.

"Sibling?".

"Deceased. Polio."

Pausing, the nurse took a pink-colored sugar cube from a silver tray. She placed it on Judy's tongue. Judy thought it tasted good.

Reassuringly the nurse said, "The vaccine has been administered."

Finally, Judy's mother relaxed her grip. With tears in her eyes, she bent down and whispered in Judy's ear.

"Enough is enough. Now the monster will never get you."

ॐ ॐ

Valeri Paxton-Steele
3rd Place

Freedom Lobster

She needed time to think, that was all. She had to get away from the fighting, the fists, the constant jabbering of insults hurled at her. When you're in it, you're too close to it. The forest for the trees, and all that. You can't see clearly. Everything has the same dull, bruise-colored tint to it.

She had a fresh shiner, and her bottom lip was all puffed out. *Great*, she thought, *lookin' like Quasimodo again. I can't do this anymore. When is enough going to be enough, hon? How much longer are you going to be his punching bag?"*

The next couple of days were clear. No work again until Monday. He wasn't home from work, yet. He would be soon, though. *Thank God, he's on graveyard shift,* she thought. It had to be now. Her mom was going to pick up the boys from school. She had the cat packed. Captain FuzzyBoots, her brindle tabby, was all set to get dropped off at her best friend's house. Charlie wouldn't care. Less mouths to feed was going to be fine by him. *Thank God, too, that those kids aren't his,* she thought again, for the zillionth time.

She grabbed the car keys, her medicines, and took a quick last look around. Inhaler, cell phone, debit card, cat. Anxious to leave, her tearful, swollen eyes quickly scanned the room. Anything else? Time was ticking, and she couldn't afford to hang around.

A quick check of the glove box assured her all the maps were there. She used to spend her "single days" doing something she jokingly referred to as "gas burning." She would drive off into nowhere, taking random lefts and rights as the mood struck her. Back then, she always picked up maps from the mini-marts and rest stops that dotted the highways.

She never cared where she ended up – that wasn't the point. The quiet was the point. No one bugging her, no one demanding anything of her. Driving was solitary bliss. That was what she needed now, more than anything else. Peace and quiet. If she didn't get some time away, she thought she would go mad. *More loco than the Mad freakin' Hatter,* she told herself.

She stocked up at the gas station a couple of blocks down from her apartment. Motor oil, dry gas, wiper fluid. They were the "just-in-case" things she considered essentials. Two waters, a couple of Slim-Jim's, a bag of chips and a full tank completed the purchase. The old clerk behind the counter, Kevin, noticed the fresh bruises. He looked worried and whispered a quick "Are you okay?" She gave him a sad smile and a slight nod.

"You didn't see me, okay, hon?"

"See who?" he joked.

With a quick gesture, she tapped the side of her nose a few times, as if to say, "We've got a secret." She winked.

She drove east all day, and most of the night. Her mind raced with all of the things that might be happening back home. This wasn't easy. She purposely powered down her phone so she wouldn't have to deal with him. It was about

12:30 in the morning when she got off the highway and pulled in to an empty McDonald's parking lot. She had been up for over 30 hours, her face hurt, and she was dead tired. She shimmied her not-so-svelte body into the backseat, and used her purse as a pillow.

When the early morning staff started to trickle in, she felt self-conscious. She could feel how swollen her face was, and one look at her reflection in the rearview mirror confirmed it. The black eye was turning lovely shades of green and purple. The "white" of her eye was red. She sure could have used a McMuffin and some coffee, and drinking all that water hadn't done her bladder any favors, but she couldn't bring herself to go in. She was just too ashamed. Better to be on the road. Guaranteed the next "comfort station" wouldn't have so many people.

She downed a couple of pain pills with the last of her lukewarm water. Hopefully, it wouldn't be long before she got to the coast. She told herself yesterday, before she left, that she was going to drive until she ran out of land. By the time she passed Danvers, she was hopeful. She could smell the salt air. The ocean wouldn't be too much farther now.

When she finally reached Rockport, it was like a huge wave of relief washed over her body. Later, she stopped at a little gas station on the outskirts of Cape Ann. She needed to "feed the tank" one more time between now and whatever destiny had in store for her at the end of this road. Hanging near the register, on proud display, were these funky, ugly (but adorable) plushy stuffed lobsters. Their blood red color was a perfect match for the "white" of her eye. She laughed and bought one. The plush toy was so absurd, so cute, she couldn't resist the purchase.

Alone on the motel patio, she looked out at the ocean. She grabbed a chair from her room, the warm blanket off the bed, and carried her "freedom lobster" outside with her. She wrapped up in the comforter and nestled in. Snuggled, all safe and secure, she watched the grey waves... storm clouds melding ocean colors with sky colors until it grew dark. In the inky blackness, the twin lighthouses captivated her attention.

The pulsing red beacon from Thacher Island was almost hypnotic. She thought about how horribly comfortable the idea of *sameness* was. Yes, it was always bad. *But, I always expected it to be bad, so there were no surprises there,* she mused. She had picked him—she deserved it—she was living with that choice—accepting the responsibility of that pick by staying—she wasn't disloyal... the thoughts came tumbling out, a dismayed swirling without rhyme or reason.

It was "The Unknown" that made life without him a whole new ballgame. *Sure, beatings are scary, but not as scary as leaving. What happens next? Poverty? Homelessness? Unemployment, maybe? Where can we go, if no one takes us in?* She cried softly to herself, gripping the lobster protectively in fierce and painful heartache. *I thought he loved me. Maybe he did, for a while. I still love him. I can't just turn it on and off like a faucet, like he does....*

Time and distance granted her exactly what she needed. She was able to gain a new perspective, crying quietly along with the battleship-grey clouds. It took some time, but she steeled herself. The issue was resolved. No matter what, she would never go back to him. Peace and calm were so very precious—and peace was all that she ever really wanted. This little lobster was tangible proof that she could survive on her own. She had the power to make her life be whatever she wanted it to be—*however* she wanted it to be. All of the choices were *hers*.

Years later, right next to her pillow, rests her salvation: a reminder of the sweet calm of peace and sanity. Her proof of a life well lived, on her own terms. Proof is something as simple as a token stuffed animal, bought on a whim, from a highway gas station somewhere off the coast of Massachusetts – her precious little freedom lobster.

Judges' Picks:

ઈ~ભ

Nonfiction

Elizabeth Davis
1st Place

Five Unique Justices of the Supreme Court

The United States Supreme Court was created by Article III of the United States Constitution in 1789. At that time, only six judges were appointed—five associate justices and one Chief Justice. The number of sitting justices has changed over the years, reaching a maximum of ten in 1863. The final change was made in 1869, which set the number of justices at nine. Only 112 men and women have served as justices on the nation's Highest Court. Here are five of the most unique of those Justices (listed in the order of their appointment) and the reason behind that distinction.

NUMBER 1: John Rutledge is the only justice to be rejected after taking the bench.

Rutledge was born a British subject on September 17, 1739, in South Carolina. He was a delegate to the First and Second Continental Congresses and was on the Committee of Detail at the Constitutional Convention of 1787.

Nominated by President George Washington in 1789, John Rutledge was one of the original six justices appointed to the United States Supreme Court. Rutledge resigned in 1791 to become Chief Justice of the South Carolina Court of Common Pleas and Sessions. When Chief Justice John Jay resigned in 1795, Washington appointed Rutledge to replace him. A recess appointment, it was five months before Congress convened. By that time, Rutledge had made a lot of enemies and his appointment was rejected. To date, he is the only justice to ever be rejected after taking the bench.

Mentally ruined, Rutledge resigned from the Supreme Court and withdrew from public life. He died on July 23, 1800.

NUMBER 2: Samuel Chase is the only Justice to be impeached.

Chase was born in Maryland on April 17, 1741. He was elected to the Maryland General Assembly in 1764 and served for 20 years. As Maryland's representative, Chase attended the First and Second Continental Congress and was one of 56 men who signed the Declaration of Independence.

In 1788, Chase was appointed Chief Justice of the District Criminal Court in Baltimore. Three years later, he was also appointed Chief Justice of the Maryland General Court. Both appointments lasted until January 1796 when President Washington appointed Chase to the United States Supreme Court.

In 1803, newly-elected President Thomas Jefferson, concerned about what he considered judiciary power-grabbing, got Congress to repeal the Judiciary Act of 1801. When Associate Justice Chase voiced his disapproval to a Baltimore grand jury, President Jefferson strongly suggested Chase should be removed from the bench. Virginia Congressman John Randolph got the House of

Representatives to charge Chase with eight articles of impeachment in 1804.

The Senate's impeachment trial began in early 1805 with Vice President Aaron Burr presiding. On March 1, 1805, Justice Samuel Chase was acquitted on all counts.

Chase continued to serve on the Supreme Court until his death on June 19, 1811.

NUMBER 3: Oliver Ellsworth chaired the committee that drafted the Judiciary Act of 1789 which created the United States Supreme Court.

Ellsworth was born in Connecticut on April 29, 1745. He represented Connecticut at the First and Second Continental Congress, serving on several committees, including the Committee of Appeals which was, for all practical purposes, the forerunner of the United States Supreme Court. Ellsworth was also a delegate to the Constitutional Convention of 1787 where he was the third future justice to serve on the Committee of Detail.

After the Constitution was ratified, Ellsworth was elected as one of Connecticut's first United States Senators and served until his appointment to the Supreme Court. Oliver Ellsworth chaired the committee for Senate Bill No. 1, the Judiciary Act, which established the United States Supreme Court.

President Washington nominated Ellsworth as Chief Justice in 1796. Ellsworth sat on the Supreme Court until September 30, 1800, when he resigned due to poor health.

Ellsworth died on November 26, 1807.

NUMBER 4: John Archibald Campbell is the only Supreme Court Justice to resign from the bench to join the Confederacy.

John A. Campbell was born in Georgia on June 24, 1811. A child prodigy, Campbell graduated from the University of Georgia at the age of 14. He immediately went to West Point for three years, but withdrew and returned to Georgia when his father died.

It took a special act of the state legislature for Campbell to be admitted to the Georgia bar in 1829, as he was only 18 years old at the time. Later he moved to Alabama and practiced there as well. By 1852, Campbell was practicing before the Supreme Court.

Campbell's nomination to the Supreme Court in 1853 was recommended to President Pierce by several sitting justices after the Senate refused three by President Fillmore in 1852. Campbell was appointed to the Supreme Court on March 21, 1853.

When states seceded from the Union, Campbell attempted to mediate between Confederate commissioners and President Lincoln, but the attempt failed. After Fort Sumter and Lincoln's call for troops, Campbell resigned from the Supreme Court on April 30, 1861. Confederate President Jefferson Davis appointed Campbell Assistant Secretary of War for the Confederacy.

In 1865, Campbell was among the delegates who tried unsuccessfully to negotiate a peaceful end to the war. After the war, Campbell was arrested and imprisoned at Fort Pulaski, Georgia. He was released after six months and returned to private practice in New Orleans where he continued to argue cases before the Supreme Court.

John Campbell died on March 12, 1889.

NUMBER 5: William Howard Taft is the only person to serve as both President and Supreme Court Justice.

Taft was born in Ohio on September 15, 1857. Starting at the local level, Taft was appointed to the Superior Court of Cincinnati in 1887. His next appointments were: Solicitor General of the US in 1890, a judge on the US Court of Appeals for the Sixth Circuit in 1891, Governor-General of the Philippines in 1900, and Secretary of War in 1904.

Taft became President in 1908 and served only one term.

On June 30, 1921, President Warren G. Harding nominated Taft Chief Justice of the Supreme Court. Taft was confirmed by the Senate and took his oath of office on July 11, 1921.

Taft resigned from the Supreme Court on February 3, 1930, due to failing health. He died less than five weeks later on March 8, 1930.

ଓ ଘ

Billie Holladay Skelley
2nd Place

The Lord Gave You a Brain to Use

As a child, I was painfully shy. I hardly spoke to anyone unless it was absolutely necessary. The one person I felt truly comfortable around was my grandmother. I liked her company because she talked a lot, and I did not have to respond often. My grandmother spoke about her past dreams, her current happenings, and her future plans. She described what she saw, what she thought, what she felt, and what she was doing. A child of the South, she had a smooth, rhythmic drawl I found captivating. To my ears, the flow of her accent was soothing. Like a gently babbling brook, I found her words relaxing and comforting. She always kept up a stream of conversation when she was around me, and looking back now, I realize she probably was trying to draw me out of my shyness and hoping to get me to be more communicative.

I never remember my grandmother shouting. She could keep your attention without raising her voice. Above all, my grandmother never swore or used any type of profanity. She felt there was absolutely no need for anyone to use "dirty" words, and she would firmly, but softly admonish anyone who did use such words in her presence. As she put it: "The Lord gave you a brain and you ought to be able to use it to find a better word to express yourself." I heard my grandmother make this statement often enough that her feelings on the matter were clear. I never ever recall her saying a "dirty" word, except on one occasion. On that particular occasion, it was highly appropriate, and it taught me an important lesson.

One thing my grandmother loved to talk about was the movies. Her favorite movie was *Gone with the Wind*, and it was special, she said, because it paired a tragic romance with a tragic time in history. The costuming, the scenery, and the expansiveness of the film attracted her. Two scenes in particular impressed her: the burning of Atlanta, and the scene where Scarlett O'Hara is looking for a doctor and walks through hundreds of injured and dead Confederate soldiers. My grandmother thought the movie was very vivid with the bright hues of the new Technicolor, and she felt the characters were so genuine in their acting that the story just came alive.

The first time I was old enough to see the movie, I enjoyed it, too. All of my grandmother's comments rang true to me, and I thought it was a great film. In time, however, I discovered a secret.

I learned, by listening very carefully to my grandmother's words, the real reason she loved the movie so much was that she thought Clark Gable was a tremendous heartthrob! In her words, Mr. Gable, who played Rhett Butler in the film, was the "cat's pajamas." She thought he was an extremely talented actor and a truly handsome man.

I remember, when I first discovered this fact, being somewhat amazed my grandmother thought another man, besides my grandfather, was so great. There was no denying, however, she thought Clark Gable was special. She considered the actor to be attractive, talented, and absolutely perfect.

Whenever *Gone with the Wind* was featured anywhere near our area, my grandmother always found the time to go to the movies. I have no idea how many times she saw the film, but she would always comment on the way Mr. Gable spoke and how he delivered his lines. She especially admired his last line in the film where he, as Rhett Butler, says to Scarlett O'Hara: "Frankly, my dear, I don't give a damn." My grandmother, however, who never swore, always amended the line to "Frankly, my dear, I don't care," but it was clear she thought Clark Gable's delivery of that line was special, dramatic, and unforgettable.

When Clark Gable died in 1960, I was still a child, but I remember my grandmother being extremely sad at his passing. She genuinely grieved and mourned his loss. From her perspective, a superstar, who had graced the world with his talents, was gone. A light had gone out in her world.

Some of my relatives, however, who did not share my grandmother's devotion to Clark Gable, thought it would be "funny" to send her a sympathy card since she thought so highly of the actor. They bought a very expensive and rather elaborate sympathy card which they promptly addressed and mailed to my grandmother. The card, which was left unsigned, conveyed in fancy script that the sender was so sorry for the loss of someone who was so close, dear, and special to her.

When my grandmother received the card, she truly thought someone in the family had passed away. She proceeded to inquire of family members, near and far, who it was that had recently died. No one offered any answers, of course, and my grandmother could not find out who the card was from or who the person was that had succumbed. She grew more and more troubled, confused, and dismayed.

After a few weeks, the guilty relatives, who had sent the card, confessed they had mailed it on behalf of the late Mr. Gable. They apologized for the inquiries and confusion it had created, but it was abundantly evident, from their tone and laughter, they enjoyed the merriment, at least from their perspective, the card had caused. They thought the whole incident had been great fun and an entertaining diversion.

My grandmother was relieved no one in the family had died, but she was also irritated and embarrassed their amusement had come at her expense. To the surprise of my young ears, she responded loudly and clearly to these family members with a slightly altered version of Rhett Butler's famous line: "Frankly, my dears, I don't give a damn. I still think he is a great actor, and I still like him!" Her delivery was every bit as vibrant and resounding as Mr. Gable's original version.

All of the guilty relatives laughed at her response, but I think my grandmother was a little embarrassed at using the real "dirty" word in front of me. I know I was shocked because my grandmother never used profanity. The fact that she had said a "dirty" word both astonished and astounded me. I am sure my mouth fell open. I think, even though I was in a state of shock, I realized for the first time the depth of her feelings for Clark Gable and what it cost her to express them.

I remember my grandmother looked at me, smiled, and said: "Sometimes you have to say what you mean and mean what you say—no matter whose ears are listening."

In that moment, my grandmother never seemed more human or more real to me. I don't think I will ever forget those words she spoke and the smile on her face as she said them. It altered the way I thought and felt about talking.

My grandmother taught me many things over the years, but on that particular day, I learned there are times you just cannot be shy and hesitant to talk. There are occasions when you have to say what you believe and stand by it. There are instances, when it is essential for you to explain how you feel—even if it is in a language or form you would not normally use. My grandmother taught me there are moments when you have to speak your mind and let the world know you are here—alive, thinking, and feeling. Simply put, I learned from my grandmother there are times when you absolutely must speak up. The smile on her face that day taught me it is often worth the effort it takes.

My grandmother passed away many years ago, but whenever I see *Gone with the Wind* on television, I think of her. When I hear Rhett Butler deliver his famous parting words to Scarlett O'Hara, I cannot help but smile and think of her altered version of that line. It always reminds me of the day, so long ago, when she taught me about the importance of communication—in whatever form it takes.

If I am honest, I have to admit I am still somewhat shy. I know now, however, there are times when you have to stand up for what you believe, speak your piece, and live with the consequences. No matter how shy you are or how much you hate public speaking, there are moments when you have to say what you mean and mean what you say—no matter who is listening or what the effect will be. When you are finished, if your words leave a smile on your face, you know it was worth it.

Thanks, Grandma. I'm still trying to use my brain to find the right words. I am still trying to communicate.

Other Contributions

శు ~ ఇ

Vicki Cox

Autumn Corpses

It's raining leaves today,
a suicidal migration
from the heart you broke.
Who could blame them?
I'd jump myself if
your silent, bony fingers
clenched my throat.
But I'm rooted here,
naked in your absence
—and theirs.
Most died on impact,
a scarlet stain
on my memory of you.
An unlucky few survived the fall.
They clatter down the street
on curling edges,
preferring
to be crushed by cars
or stacked in mass graves
beside the curb,
useful to no one
except dogs with lifted legs
and the hopeful who like diving into trash.

What shall I say about the toast?

It was a fresh bread morning,
when rain wet maple seeds clung to the grass,
when faded aprons, cracked breadboards,
and knuckle-thickened hands,
converged at the vinyl blue tablecloth
punching, folding, slapping
dough that rose like hope
under the dish towel.
Two loaves baked in battered pans,
one for eating,
the other, cellophane wrapped,
for giving away.

I bite,
the crust awakes my tongue,
its tender core,
collapsing between teeth.
I greet the jelly,
a smear,
not enough to spoil the wait
for butter pooling in the pores.

But then,
near the end,
I am jarred by char,
abrading the underside,
a scorch across my reverie,
an insult so heinous to love,
I prefer the bitter burn of coffee
to wash its ashes away.

What shall I say about the toast you gave me?

The diet

It was too much,
love gone soft.
cracked shells,
slipping, sliding, breaking off
our vanilla world.
It filled me up,
puffed me out,
like too much ice cream
licked too slowly
down sticky trails.
Your strawberry grit filled my thoughts
and weighed me down,
like too many all-you-can-eat noon buffets
on Sunday afternoons.

Now,
in these lean, hard days
stretched taunt and spare,
I run portion controlled,
calorie counted,
fat free,
overfull of negatives,
ever mindful
not to wish,
not to long,
not to hope,
not to think
of you.

Thumbs Up

By chance
silver rises,
head over tails
beyond the grasp of reason.
A toss up of
hope or fear
pearl or ebony
full moon or half dome.
Greek gods
vault midnight's
thunderstorms to rest on heaven's urn
or cinched
into Dante's black pouch
where guitars weep and
sightless faces wait in jars.
It's a Russian split
where the marble stops
or the quarter falls.
You make the call
It's up to you
while I fall
end over end, helplessly,
to the ground.

Pale Riders

No one noticed.
certainly not
wide-eyed deer,
cowering in the brush
after gravel cracked
under their feet,
nor fishermen casting
dreams in the dark,
nor teens hidden in the trees,
fogging pick-up windows
with new love
(or maybe just lust).
But last night
we skated to heaven's rim
on silver blades forged by last quarter's
moon.
A spray of constellations
settled in our wake,
fire and ice coupled,
too hot to hold
too cold to taste.

Hands veined with light
held thunderstorms at bay
while we teetered on
midnight's edge,
undecided
if falling on its cusp
was suicide
or a mere blood letting
of old love
still festering in
reunited hearts.

છ જી

Anita Crews

The Lad and the Dragon
(A Sestina)

Let me tell you a story
It's a very long tale
About a lad who was daring
He had courage to spare
Those who heard it cried
No one could rest, so loudly they wept.

So loudly they wept
As I told the lad's story
The girls cried
As I got to the tale
About courage to spare
A yarn, a saga, of daring.

A dragon bold and daring
Many wept,
As no person would he spare
As I was told the story
I now relate the tale.
People were alarmed and cried

As he marched to face the dragon he cried,
But the lad went bravely on, still daring.
Many covered their ears, so not to hear the tale.
The girls huddled together and wept.
The troubadour remembered the story
Of the lad with a sword and courage to spare

He met the dragon, and with courage to spare
He stood up to the dragon and cried
"It will be the end of your story
For I am full of daring,
Before the finish you will have wept.
It will be the end of your tale."

It became quite a yarn, quite a tale
Of the lad who had courage to spare
The boy severed a dragon's toe; the dragon wept.
The tears put out the fire, when the dragon cried.
That's how a lad filled with daring,
Ended fear of the dragon, so I can tell the story.

It's the end of the story, the end of the tale
Of a lad filled with daring and courage to spare.
The people cheered and cried; the old dragon wept.

      ઠ ઝ

Elizabeth Davis

The Supreme Court and Its Journey to Nine Justices

The Constitution of the United States was written in 1787, ratified in 1788, and became effective March 4, 1789.

Article III, Section 1 of the Constitution says, "The judicial Power of the United States, shall be vested in one supreme Court, and in such inferior Courts as the Congress may from time to time ordain and establish. The Judges, both of the supreme and inferior Courts, shall hold their Offices during good Behavior, and shall, at stated Times, receive for their Services, a Compensation, which shall not be diminished during their Continuance in Office."

The composition and procedures of the courts were left to Congress.

The Supreme Court began with 6 Justices

Judiciary Act of 1789, September 24, 1789, 1 Stat. 73

"An Act to establish the Judicial Courts of the United States."

The Judiciary Act of 1789 established the court system of the United States and set the number of justices on the Supreme Court at six.

Section 1: Be it enacted by the Senate and House of Representatives of the United States of America in Congress assembled, **That the supreme court of the United States shall consist of a chief justice and five associate justices**, any four of whom shall be a quorum, and shall hold annually at the seat of government two sessions, the one commencing the first Monday of February, and the other the first Monday of August. That the associate justices shall have precedence according to the date of their commissions, or when the commissions of two or more of them bear date on the same day, according to their respective ages.

Congress also set the times and location of the sessions along with other necessary details.

The Supreme Court was decreased to 5 Justices

Judiciary Act of 1801, February 13, 1801, 2 Stat. 89

"An Act to provide for the more convenient organization of the Courts of the United States."

The next Judiciary Act was passed on February 13, 1801, and is largely overlooked by historians. This Act reduced the number of justices to five—or rather, it would have, had it not been repealed so soon after enactment.

Section 3: <u>And be it further enacted, That from and after the next vacancy that shall happen in the said court, it shall consist of five justices only; that is to say, of one chief justice, and four associate justices.</u>

The Supreme Court was returned to 6 Justices

Judiciary Act of 1802, March 8, 1802, 2 Stat. 132

"An Act to repeal certain acts respecting the organization of the Courts of the United States; and for other purposes."

Barely a year had passed before Congress repealed the Judiciary Act of 1801 which effectively kept the number of justices at six.

Section 1: Be it enacted by the Senate and House of Representatives of the United States of America in Congress assembled, That the act of Congress passed on the thirteenth day of February one thousand eight hundred and one, intituled "An Act to provide for the most convenient organization of the courts of the United States," from and after the first day of July next, shall be, and is hereby repealed.

A second Judiciary Act of 1802 was passed on April 29, 1802, 2 Stat. 156, which re-instated much of the original Judiciary Act of 1801, but made no change to the number of justices on the bench.

The Supreme Court was increased to 7 Justices

Establishment of the Seventh Circuit, February 24, 1807, 2 Stat. 420

"An Act establishing Circuit Courts, and abridging the jurisdiction of the district courts of Kentucky, Tennessee and Ohio."

The next change to the judicial system and the number of justices on the Supreme Court occurred on February 24, 1807, when Congress established a seventh circuit.

Section 5: Be it further enacted, **That the supreme court of the United States shall hereafter consist of a chief justice, and six associate justices**, any law to (the) contrary notwithstanding. And for this purpose there shall be appointed a sixth associate justice, to reside in the seventh circuit, whose duty it shall be, until he is otherwise allotted, to attend the circuit courts of the said seventh circuit, and the supreme court of the United States, and who shall take the same oath, and be entitled to the same salary as are required of, and provided for the other associate justices of the United States.

The Supreme Court was increased to Nine Justices

Establishment of the Eighth and Ninth Circuits, March 3, 1837, 5 Stat. 176

"An Act supplementary to the act entitled 'An act to amend the judicial system of the United States.'"

Thirty years went by before Congress made another change to the Supreme Court. With the establishment of two more circuits in 1837, the number of justices on the bench also increased by two.

Section 1: "Be it enacted, by the Senate and House of Representatives of the United States of America in Congress assembled, **That the Supreme Court of the United States shall hereafter consist of a chief justice, and eight associate judges**, any five of whom shall constitute a quorum; and for this purpose there shall be appointed two additional justices of said court, with the like powers, and to take the same oaths, perform the same duties, and be entitled to the same salary, as the other associate judges."

The Supreme Court peaks at 10 Justices

Establishment of the Tenth Circuit, March 3, 1863, 12 Stat. 794

"An Act to provide Circuit courts for the Districts of California and Oregon, and for other Purposes."

The next change to the Supreme Court occurred during the War Between the States. With the addition of the Tenth Circuit, Congress added one more justice to the Supreme Court.

Section 1: Be it enacted by the Senate and House of Representatives of the United States of America in Congress assembled, **That the supreme court of the United States shall hereafter consist of a chief justice and nine associate justices**, any six of whom shall constitute a quorum; and for this purpose there shall be appointed one additional associate justice of said court, with the like powers, and to take the same oaths, perform the same duties, and be entitled to the same salary, as the other associate justices. The districts of California and Oregon shall constitute the tenth circuit, and the other circuits shall remain as now constituted by law.

Congress cuts the Supreme Court to 7 Justices

Reorganization of the Judicial circuits, July 23, 1866, 14 Stat. 209

"An Act to fix the Number of Judges of the Supreme Court of the United States, and to change certain Judicial Circuits."

After the assassination of President Abraham Lincoln, Vice President Andrew Johnson stepped into the Presidency. In order to keep the Southern President from appointing anyone to the Supreme Court, Congress reduced the number of justices to seven.

Section 1: Be it enacted by the Senate and House of Representatives of the United States of America in Congress assembled, **That no vacancy in the office of associate justice of the supreme court shall be filled by appointment until the number of associate justices shall be reduced to six; and thereafter the said supreme court shall consist of a chief justice of the United States and six associate justices**, any four of whom shall be a quorum; and the said court shall hold one term annually at the seat of government, and such adjourned or special terms as it may find necessary for the despatch of business.

Congress returned the Supreme Court to 9 Justices

Judiciary Act of 1869, April 10, 1869, 16 Stat. 44

"An Act to amend the Judicial System of the United States."

For the third time in a decade, Congress passed an act changing the number of justices on the Supreme Court. After Ulysses S. Grant replaced Johnson as President, Congress returned the Court to nine justices.

Section 1: Be it enacted by the Senate and House of Representatives of the United States of America in Congress assembled, **That the Supreme Court of the United States shall hereafter consist of the Chief Justice of the United States and eight associate justices**, any six of whom shall constitute a quorum; and for the purposes of this act there shall be appointed an additional associate justice of said court.

Summary

Congress changed the number of justices on the Supreme Court seven times between 1789 and 1869. Although many judiciary acts have been passed during the past 148 years, the number of justices on the Court has remained at nine.

Gail Denham

Mr. Blanding Builds His Dream House

If Cary Grant hadn't got locked
in that new house closet, Milt might
have quit watching the movie.

Struck Milt funny, a grown man
couldn't fight his way out of a closet
in that halfway-built fancy house,
what with his good looks and the money
he made pretending on screen.

"Who needs such a big house anyways,"
Milt said. "We got all we need—indoor
plumbing, a gas stove, and a garage for my
car. We even got us a black and white TV."

His wife Sophie hitched up her front, smoothed
her slightly flour-streaked apron with the blue
flowers and murmured. "One day 'twould make
life easy could we get a real washer that don't
threaten to grab and smash my hand in the wringer
on wash days. And maybe a toaster for bread that
ain't scorched black over a burner, while I try hard
not to set my fingers on fire."

The Meaning of Bears on a Boat

Fishing was good that day. Two twelve inchers in the creel. We came to the shallow part of Ramble Creek. This section was wade deep. Evening crept swift from the west. Water so cold it near froze our catch, floating behind. Little sand and gravel islands caused Ben to paddle around them. From a thicket of tall willow came the bear, charging and splashing as if she had a personal beef with fisher persons.

Next thing we knew, we wuz in the water. I never felt icier. A huge Kodiak planted paws inside our boat. She half leaned on the motor casing, pulled those two big ones off our line, fixin' to enjoy a picnic. Wondered if I should offer her some tartar sauce, or head for a tree. The boat hung up on a gravel spit. Bear settled back to enjoy her catch.

My legs became wooden froze. Ben and I sloshed to the bank. We'd wait her out. Meanwhile Ben found the dry match pack and we gathered wood.

We glared at our brown intruder. "Elmer warned us about this here stretch," Ben growled. "Said there was danger of all sort." I grunted and scootched closer to the fire. On the creek, the boat broke free. Friend bear kept eating. Our craft, with everything aboard sped up a little, headed round a curve.

About five minutes later, we heard two sharp "cracks." Someone had taken advantage of our floating target. We took off running, hoping the hunter didn't think the boat came with his kill. As we ran, I imagined the tale this sharp shooter would tell round his campfire that night. "And here come this bear, driving his own boat."

Love on the Line

They met atop a pole, stringing wire, pounding staples. A real connection, except he dropped his hammer. Thump! Sadie was tempted to laugh. Ray groaned, smiled and asked to borrow her equipment.

That afternoon, over snacks at the truck, Ray smiled again. "Always been a klutz. How about racing up the next pole? Winner buys dinner."

Sadie, only months out of a bad relationship, somehow couldn't say no.

They'd been assigned the Eastern Oregon poles. Cold! Sadie shivered, but agreed to bet. As they belted up, she watched Ray. He was cute, in a farm-boy way. They'd probably have a meal at the local greasy spoon. A change from the dud she'd dated. Chad wanted the best. Finally, she wasn't good enough. One reason she'd taken this job— a total change.

She liked real people. Ray even walked bow-legged. Probably grew up riding horses. She'd love to ride.

"Oops," Sadie yelped, midway up the pole. "Dropped my staple gun. You win."

Ray grinned, kept climbing. "Don't forget our dinner bet."

Sadie started the truck engine. Country music. "Home again," crooned the singer. She watched Ray finish their job.

Dinner was at a small cafe. "How's the burger?" Ray asked.

"Delish," Sadie said. "I'm full." However, she eyed the berry pie, her favorite. Great hamburgers, scrumptious pie, and locals chatting it up around them.

Ray was quiet. She liked that too. She peppered him with questions. Sure enough, horses were a big part of his life. "We raised Arabians," Ray said. "Wanted to race them. Only had some exciting endurance runs."

Sadie told herself Ray was simply interesting, she didn't intend to become involved. Her lineman job was temporary until she discovered a career. She had computer training. She hated offices, but that might be next.

They dated several months while they worked that east pole line—movies, diners, a local theater group. One night, in Ray's pickup, he asked, "Want to visit my folks' farm?"

"You bet," she exclaimed. "I was raised in suburbia. Do they still have animals?"

"Sure. Several horses, a few cows; chickens everywhere, plus three dogs, two cats."

Sadie laughed. "Sounds lively."

Ray blushed. "Actually, I'm living with my folks till I get an apartment. Not easy around here. I'm going to start a business." Sadie sighed. So, he planned to stay here.

"What kind of business?" she inquired.

"Have a degree in computer technology; I'll do consulting and repair," Ray said.

His folks were great. The meal his mom served was over the top. Roast so tender she fork-cut it; carrot cake with real whipped cream. However, the best part, afterwards, relaxing on the wood porch swing with Ray.

He worked as fast as he climbed poles—pulled her close. "Tomorrow we'll go for a ride. Up for that? She could only nod as his mouth covered hers. Sadie hadn't planned on this "connection" but suddenly her heart promised she'd found someone who was more than a pole climber, someone down to earth.

Between the Lines

As she writes, her tears dot the page; her between-the-lines message clear—she hugs her pillow at night, so tight her fingers go numb; she says "Robbie cries," doesn't say that Robbie sometimes forgets who is the man in the photo beside the radio, where they gather nightly to hear if anyone speaks hope.

Penned in correct cursive, rain drops dot his letter to her, or is it tears? Willie writes to Lois from France, dated 1943, unknown location, sent free by military mail.

He tells "I take a bath in my helmet, not bad if I have soap"—but doesn't say the jeep ahead of him hit a land mine and his friend's body parts splattered his windshield. Nor does he mention his feet, swollen because there's no time to dry sox.

Does she understand his between-the-lines longing for their Sunday chicken dinners at the oak table, or his desire to hold her and little Robbie for just five minutes?

But not now. They pile on fighting gear, check rifles, grab C-Rations and a canteen, store letters in duffels, pray to come back safe; all because he embraces his duty, believes they must win to protect loved ones. They head out for another foray into dark doorways, alleys, or intense woods with trees so tight, they don't see an enemy, only the flash.

He doesn't tell her that. Between-the-lines, she reads love, feels his fear. She can almost hear his voice. He pens,

"Write often dearest. Your letters are my bright spot. Kiss Robbie—don't let him forget me. I love you. Gotta go. Send cookies."

Meanwhile, back across the world, she begins another letter. "Dearest Willie. Today Robbie decided to scrub all his toy trucks in the tub..."

Drying Lard

Backed against the counter, Ann
reached behind her for the skillet.
It was still hot, filled with bacon
grease, which made lovely lines
of drying lard on Richard's
dark gray suit.

Diane L. Kehres

Every Wednesday

Angie felt her heart rate slacken; her breath no longer came in gasps. Lying on her back, she reached over, placed her palm on Peter's chest. Sweat moistened her fingertips. The beat of his heart thumped against her hand. "You weren't your usual self today. Everything okay?" She turned her head to glance his way. A frown formed on his forehead, he pinched his lips together.

"No," he said. "Nothing is okay. Nothing at all."

She sat up in bed. Her unabashed nakedness always aroused him. This time, he didn't take notice. "Want to talk about it?"

"In a minute. Let's dress first." He rolled away from her. A silent stone.

"Fine by me. Mind if I use the john?" Rather than wait for a reply, she gathered her undies, walked by his side of the bed, paused and faced him. Full frontal. No response. No eye contact. Not even a shrug. How long had they been meeting in this swank hotel, every week on Wednesday afternoons? Six months? Eight months? She sauntered to the bathroom, closed the door with a gentle snap.

When she returned, she found him perched on the side of the bed. Fully clothed. Except for shoes. The jacket to his thousand-dollar suit lay folded on the bed next to him. She put on her gray silk blouse, leisurely buttoned it, then shimmied the black pencil skirt over her hips, slid her feet into heels. "You in a hurry today, Judge?"

"Angie, I'm going back to my wife." He turned his gaze her way. They eyed each other, neither in a rush to break the stare.

"Hand me my hairbrush, sweetie. It's in my bag. There on the table."

"Did you hear what I said?" he asked. He rummaged through the expansive leather bag. Pulled out a realistic flesh-tone vibrator. He held it toward her. "Not a hairbrush."

"Oh, I brought that in case we needed a little extra incentive. Dig a little further. I can't brush my hair with that." He produced the hairbrush, handed it to her, and replaced the incentive back in the bag.

"When did you decide this? I didn't think that was an option." As she stood in front of the mirror, drawing the brush through her hair, she watched him struggle to form words.

"I've been thinking about it for some time." He let out a sigh. "For God's sake, Angie, Martha and I have been married for thirty years. I won't throw that away."

"Certainly not. I wouldn't expect you to. Perhaps I'm too much of a distraction for you." She ambled his way, reached for her bag, retrieved a tube of lipstick and perfume. She patted him on the cheek. "However, I can guarantee you, Martha won't do the things I do for you. Not from what you told me." Back at the mirror, she applied the red to her lips, spritzed the fine musky mist over her wrists and deep in her cleavage. "Maybe that's the way you want it." Retrieving her jacket from the back of a chair, she draped it over her arm, went to the bed, and sat beside him."

"I'm sorry, but that's the way things need to be. Neither one of us expected this to go on forever, did we?"

Angie reached for his hand, and held it tight in her own. "No, I suppose not. My only concern is that we still have to work together. Will there be a problem the next time I show up in your court room?"

"Of course not. We're both professionals." A slight tremor developed in his hand as she held it.

She released his hand, pushed her arms into the sleeves of her jacket, and stood. "Sounds good to me." She clutched her bag and fished out her phone. Her fingers nimbly worked the keyboard. "I've removed you from my calendar. So, we're done."

"That was too easy, Angie."

"I see no reason to make things adversarial. As you said, our only commitment was for Wednesdays, one to two. Nothing more. I'm fine with that."

"I expected you might make more of a fuss, be put off by the whole thing." The Judge stood and donned his own jacket. Worked his feet into loafers. Crossed over to the mirror to adjust his tie. A jet engine roared overhead, a planeload of commuters off to some spot other than this one.

"Does she know about me? Is that what this is about?" Angie stepped toward the door.

"No. And I'd prefer to keep it that way."

"You'll get no argument from me." She reached for the doorknob, paused. "One last kiss?" Shifting her bag from one shoulder to the other, she caressed his neck, and brushed her lips over his cheek. He tasted of sweat salt with a hint of aftershave. She used her thumb to rub away the scarlet kiss that lingered on his cheek. "Good bye, Peter. Take care of yourself." A red smile flashed his way. "See you in court."

Angie opened the door, stepped into the hall. The door shut with a sucking click. She made her way to the elevator. A quick bell signaled the arrival of the car. The doors whooshed open. Alone; she was the sole passenger. The elevator made its descent as the slightest hint of a tear formed in one eye. She blinked it away when the doors opened onto the lobby.

"*C'est la vie*. Win some. Lose some. There are plenty more where he came from. Next time I'll look for one who doesn't have a noose around his neck."

Angie left the building, summoned the valet to fetch her Mercedes ragtop. While she waited, the warm spring breeze fluttered against her skin. The Judge exited from the same door she had passed through a few moments before. Neither spoke. Nor glanced in the other's direction. Strangers waiting for cars in front of a five-star hotel. Hers came first. She tipped the valet, got in, and drove away. A hole in her calendar. A hole in her heart.

A Gathering of Friends

Evelyn adjusted her jacket, gathering its front edge together with her fists, hoping to ward off the chilled air that hurled into the room every time the door to the tiny French café opened. Since it was happy hour, the door welcomed the draft often. At fifty-eight, she considered herself a no-nonsense type of woman—brown hair streaked with gray, dark-rimmed glasses, minimal makeup, just a little mascara, blush, and lipstick. Thirty years of teaching English lit to undergrads at the local university helped keep her trim, and on her toes. Open to possibility.

The cool draft on her feet announced a newcomer. A warm smile graced her face as she stood to wave at James, the love of her life. He nodded and made his way to her table. Evelyn admired the way he carried his not-quite six-foot frame. They embraced, kissed cheeks and he took the chair next to her.

"It's sure festive in here. Reminds me of how we used to deck the halls at our house," James said. As he pulled his arms from his wool coat, he glanced around the café.

"Yes. All the holly, fresh pine, Poinsettias. Fond memories, huh?"

"Always. Fond indeed." The smile he gave when he peered into Evelyn's eyes made her feel grateful to be near him.

"How was court today?" Asking James about his day was a highlight. His pale blue eyes brightened when he shared his victories.

"We won. Case was all hot air. Never should have made it as far as it did." He placed his arm around her shoulder as he leaned back in his chair.

"Is that mole on your cheek larger?" She glanced his way and reached for a menu.

"No, I don't think so." He fingered the area in question. "It's not a problem as long as I keep the razor away from it," he said, adding a wink in her direction for added assurance.

Frigid air rushed through the open door, followed by Sara and Edward. Evelyn waved her welcome.

"Hi you two. Look who I found lurking about outside," Sara said. Her long, golden hair tumbled from the hot-pink knitted cap she pulled from her head.

"I was not lurking." A brief frown appeared on Edward's forehead. "I couldn't remember if this was the right place, that's all." He blew kisses across the table, then helped Sara with her bulky jacket.

"Like my scarf and hat?" No wait for a response. "I'm knitting one for each of you. Homemade is always the best, don't you think?" She wore a crooked grin on her face as she glanced from one to the other. "Try to be surprised. That's all I ask." She added a husky laugh. "Have you ordered?"

"No." James searched his pockets. "Let me use your readers, Evelyn."

She removed hers from her face and relinquished them to him. "I've never known you to have your glasses when you need them. You never change." The friends had a laugh at James' expense, his being the jolliest.

"I love the aromas in this place," Edward said. "I'm reminded of something. I can't remember what it is, but I love it. Makes me hungry." He helped himself to a menu, which he shared with Sara.

"It's the fresh-baked bread and the butter," Sara said, without looking away from the menu. "They sauté everything in mounds of butter."

A hush fell over the four-some as they scanned the menus. Group decision prevailed. A charcuterie platter fit the bill. Small plates of cheese, fruit, sausage, baguettes to share. Four glasses of wine clinked as James contributed a toast.

"To the liveliest group of Boomers I know. Cheers!"

"You know I'm not quite in that demographic," Edward said, a sly grin forming on his unlined face. He reached for James, but did not make contact. Good friends are the best company to share gossip with and laughter came easily. The plates emptied, glasses drained, farewells loomed.

"What time tomorrow for Christmas Eve brunch?" Edward asked. He brushed a few breadcrumbs from his yellow cashmere sweater.

"Let's say eleven-ish," Evelyn replied. She raised her eyebrows and glanced at Sara, brushed her shoulder against James' arm.

"We always used to do twelve." James met Evelyn's chestnut eyes with his own. His eyes wide, lips pinched at the edges.

"Back then, we did lots of things differently, James. A lifetime ago. When we were married." She gave a slight shake to her head. "Now things are different."

"They most certainly are." Sara leaned forward, her eyes riveted to the face of her friend's former husband.

Edward cleared his throat. "Well, we should be off. I still have presents to wrap." He stood.

James rose from his seat, paused, placed a gentle kiss on Evelyn's cheek. "We'll see you in the morning. Remember, we're bringing wine and Edward made scones."

"Great. Be careful out. It's been snowing since we got here." She watched the two men step to the door, arms linked. A last glance, a gush of cold air, and they were gone.

"Honestly, Evie, I sometimes think you still pine for James," Sara said.

"No. Not at all. It's just that old habits are hard to break." She shrugged as she gathered her coat and mittens.

"Somehow, I'm not convinced." Sara pulled the pink cap down over her ears. "You've come a long way since all this started."

"Of course, I still care for James. Just not in the same way. Besides, I'm dating Jon. A new chapter."

"Okay. As long as you're all right. All of this came as quite a jolt it seems to me."

"I'm fine, but I'm not sure I could have gotten through all this without your friendship."

"A friend comes to your aide in the time of a crisis. That's how it should be." The zipper on her jacket stalled; she yanked it loose. "I'm glad I could be there for you. What you went through, well, I couldn't have done it with such grace."

"Let's change the subject," Evelyn's smile spread to her eyes as she searched Sara's face. "It will be fun walking home in the snow."

They darted out of the café, the snow flurried in their faces. The ones with the lingering smiles.

"Life is amazing, isn't it?" Sara asked.

"Yes, amazing and wonderful."

"Let's have a merry Christmas, Evelyn."

"The merriest, Sara."

Snowflakes filled in the prints made by their boots as the two neighbors marched toward their homes. A new future beckoned. Evelyn desired love, and her determination filled her being. She found it impossible to resist uttering to the wind—"Merry Christmas Everyone."

෫ ෪

Frank Montagnino

Seasons

It was still dark when Ramón Flores rolled out of bed and slid into the pair of jeans he had hung carefully over the back of the chair near the bed. It was the same pair he'd worn since Monday and would continue to wear until Saturday while he sowed his fields. It wasn't that Ramón was slovenly. Indeed, when not working he was generally fastidious. But this was planting season and there was just no sense in dirtying up clothes needlessly, especially when he was unlikely to see another soul until the weekend.

His pants hanging loose around his still lean waist, Ramón shuffled across the cold linoleum floor to light the burner under the coffee pot on the gas stove. On the way, he tested various parts of his body to see what hurt this morning. At seventy-eight, he had to admit, something always hurt, especially after plowing or other hard work on the small farm. Today only his shoulder ached, a minor annoyance that would work itself out in the morning sun.

While the coffee perked, Ramón conducted the usual morning ritual. He tested the blade on the old straight razor he'd inherited when his father died. He stropped the blade back and forth on the leather strap hanging on the back of the bathroom door. Satisfied the blade was honed precisely, he splashed some water in his shaving mug and vigorously twirled the brush, working up a good lather which he practically ground into his salt and pepper beard. It was an old-fashioned way of shaving he knew, but it made him feel clean. Besides, he rationalized, why spend money on razor blades when his straight blade had already lasted nearly a century? His wife, Celestina had bought him several modern razors over the years trying to "bring him into the twentieth century," as she termed it. He had tried them to make her feel good, but after a week or so had always gone back to the blade.

The sun was beginning to appear over the horizon by the time Ramón had gotten dressed and had a cup of coffee along with a piece of bread left over from last night's supper. Ramón ate better breakfasts when Celestina was there to cook them, but he hadn't had ham or bacon since she passed away some eighteen years ago. He liked bread, especially coated with butter on both sides. And there were always plenty of eggs around. When he was finished eating there was only a cup, spoon and knife to wash up. He left them in the drain on the sink along with the fork which he'd use for supper. He seldom even put the utensils back in the drawer anymore. Without his sweetheart, Celestina, or any visitors, there was no need for such formalities.

Ramón shrugged into his denim jacket and stepped out onto the porch just as the rooster cut loose with his morning greeting. He walked across the sparse grass yard to the small barn where he stored his feed and seed. He took the unlocked padlock out of the rusty hasp and stepped inside. Two 60-pound burlap bags rested on the dirt floor. Ramón dug into one of them with a ten-gallon pail, filling it about half full. He took a leather bag similar to a mailman's pouch off a peg and filled it full of seed corn from the other sack. He hefted the bag over his shoulder, picked up the pail and walked out of the barn and over to the adjacent feed lot. The rooster and a flock of hens anticipated his arrival, strutting over to the fence and milling about impatiently. Ramón scattered the feed, tossing it by the handful over the fence. When the pail was empty he hung it by the handle over a fence post. He paused for a moment, leaning on the top rail of the wooden fence. He enjoyed feeding his chickens. He liked listening to their clucking. He found it soothing.

Twenty-five hundred miles away, another Ramón Flores stopped pacing and dropped into a well-worn leather chair in the waiting room of the maternity ward at St. Ignatius Hospital, Brooklyn, New York. He looked at his watch for the hundredth time since they'd checked in. Nine o'clock. It would be six in the morning in California and he knew his grandfather would be up and about. He punched in a speed dial number on his cell. Standing by the fence watching his chickens, the old man felt his phone vibrate. He fished it out of his pocket. "Hello?"

"Hey, *Abuelo*, Grandpa, it's me, Ramón. Good morning."

The old man smiled at the sound of his grandson's voice. "Good morning Niño, how are you? And how is that beautiful little lady of yours?"

"Little?" He laughed. "Carmen's as big as a barn, Gramps, but she's fine. Tired, though. She'd like to have this over with. In fact, we're at the hospital now."

"The hospital! Is everything all right?"

"Everything's fine. Today's the day, Grandpa. Today we make you a *great* grandfather."

"That's wonderful, Ramón. I just wish your father could be here to see this glorious day."

"Me too, Grandpa. You know we're going to name him after pop, keep the tradition going."

"Enrique Ramón Flores," the old man tried the name on his tongue. "It sounds good. Your dad would be proud."

"What are you doing today, Gramps?" the young Ramón asked.

"Planting corn, Niño. Have to get these seeds in the ground." He shifted the leather bag on his shoulder. *Mi Dios*, he thought, it seemed heavy this morning.

"Well, listen," the younger Ramón said, "keep your phone handy and I'll call you as soon as little Enrique arrives."

"You had better," the old man warned. "Give my love to Carmen. I love you, Ramón."

"Love you too, gramps. You take it easy now."

Ramón carefully put the phone into a pocket in his denim jacket. He shifted the leather bag into a more comfortable position and set out for the field.

The sun was well up into the sky now, but the morning chill had not yet burned off. Still, nippy as it was, he was sweating by the time he'd made the short walk to the small field. He rested for a moment. Strangely, he was more tired now at the beginning of the day, than he had been yesterday after a day of plowing. Must be getting old, he thought.

He took his phone from the denim jacket and transferred it to his pants pocket then took off the jacket and draped it over the fence rail. Ducking under the top rail he stepped through the fence, picked up his bag of seed and started slowly up the first row, dropping a single kernel every pace. It was a small field, but the planting would take all day.

Dr. Ricardo Sanchez looked to be the same age as Ramón Flores. In truth, he was ten years older and had delivered many babies. He came through the automatic doors to the maternity ward and caught Ramón's eye. "Good morning, Ray."

Ramón bounded to his feet and grabbed the doctor's outstretched hand. "Good morning, Doc."

"Just wanted you to know we're moving Carmen into Delivery. She's doing great."

"How much longer do you think, Doc?"

The doctor chuckled, "hard to say exactly, but I wouldn't think it'll take too much longer. I'll have someone tell you when the baby starts coming."

"Thanks, Doctor. I'd appreciate that."

Doctor Sanchez punched Ramón playfully on the arm and went back through the maternity ward door. Ramón slumped back in his chair and picked up a ragged, two-year-old copy of *People* magazine.

He had made only two trips slogging up and down the field and he was already winded. Hard going in this soft earth, he told himself, stopping to catch his breath. The sun had begun to beat down, but oddly, the old man felt cold. He wished he hadn't left his jacket hanging on the fence. His sore shoulder hadn't loosened up either. In fact, it felt a little worse as though the pain was radiating down his arm. He squinted up at the sun and remembered how Celestina would rub his aches away. He shifted the seed bag to his other shoulder and started up another row.

The nurse had come through the automatic doors a few minutes ago to tell Ramón the baby was coming and assure him everything was fine. Carmen was doing beautifully, she said, and it probably wouldn't be much longer. Although he knew it was a caricature of expectant fathers Ramón couldn't keep himself from pacing. He wished he'd bought some cigars, but Hell, nobody smokes anymore. Besides, they'd probably throw him out of the hospital if he lit up a stogie.

The old man had just finished another row when the pain hit him like a thunderclap. It seared him from his jaw across his chest and down his arm. He stumbled to his knees in the soft earth. He tried to think if he'd ever felt a pain so intense, but couldn't recall anything. Using his still good arm for support he slowly lowered himself until he was lying on his back in the dirt. Perhaps if he rested for a moment.

Enrique Ramón Flores came into the world with a full complement of fingers and toes and a perfectly functioning set of lungs. Carmen Flores although exhausted, saw her beautiful baby and instantly forgave her husband for putting her through all this.

As for Ramón, he was on cloud nine. He kissed his wife and all the nurses in the delivery room, then got acquainted with his new son, nestled securely in Carmen's arms. The nurses eventually pried the baby away from the new parents and took him away to be swaddled and introduced to the other newbies in the nursery. Her adrenaline depleted, Carmen needed sleep so the nurses shooed Ramón back into the waiting room where he shook hands with everyone he could find before dropping into a chair and reaching for his cell phone. He punched in his grandfather's number.

Ramón Flores felt the phone more than he heard it. Slowly he dug into his pocket and extracted the phone. He thumbed the "talk" button and tried to raise the phone to his ear, but couldn't seem to lift his arm. He didn't hear his grandson's excited voice coming through the speaker.

"Grandpa?" young Ramón called, sensing the connection had been made. "Grandpa, Enrique is here. Carmen is fine and you're a great grandpa now. Grandpa?"

Lying in the soft earth, looking up at the azure sky, Ramón Flores couldn't hear his grandson, but he was pleased to make out a misty image formed out of the puffy clouds; his love Celestina, cradling a tiny *Niño*.

The sun was warm and somehow the pain was gone. The planting could wait a few minutes while he took a short nap. A small smile creased Ramón's leathery face as he closed his eyes.

Comin' Home

August 5, 1863

Dear Ma and Pap,

It has been a month now since the big set-to here in Gettysburg and I am just now able to set pencil to paper to tell you all about it. New troops who arrive here say the news reports back home call it "The Battle of Gettysburg." I've never seen anything like it and I've seen more in my short eighteen years than most folks who get put in the ground in their seventies or eighties.

Why even the first salvo was spectacular because the line of howitzers and 12 lb. Napoleons stretched almost two miles from south of Gettysburg to the ridge we were trying to take. The noise was Godawful. Some troops around me just couldn't stand it. They just dropped to the ground with their hands over their ears and lay there despite officers kicking at them and screaming for them to 'by God get up and fight.' I wrapped a scarf around my head and that helped deaden the noise, but not by much.

The noise from the batteries was like rolling thunder, but there was also a piercing, shrill noise when shot and shell came whistling by too close. And there were huge explosions when a shell would land near our position. It would rattle your teeth, that's certain. Didn't matter who had shot it either, North or South. And then, of course there was the screaming and the moaning. I doubt I'll ever rid that horrible sound from my head.

Oh, and I almost forgot about the smoke. With so much

cannon and rifle fire on both sides the gun smoke over the field was so thick you could scarcely breathe. It was hard to see, too. You'd be stumbling forward almost blind from the smoke and the tears in your eyes, and then the smoke would part and like as not you'd find yourself staring at some blue belly rubbing his own eyes. I was lucky several times that day because I managed to get off the first shot.

But maybe I'm getting ahead of myself here. As you folks know, I'm with the 14th Virginia under Colonel James Hodges. Our bunch is a part of Armistead's Brigade in Pickett's Division of the Army of Northern Virginia. The whole shooting match is commanded by General Robert E. Lee.

According to the officers in our unit, this whole Battle of Gettysburg thing started because General Lee wanted to send a message that the Confederacy wasn't to be trifled with by pushing up into Northern territory. Heck, we didn't even know where we were headed until word came back down the column that we'd just crossed into Pennsylvania. That was kind of exciting because I'd never before been out of Virginia in all my eighteen years. Whoa! Better make that nineteen years. I almost forgot I had a birthday a couple of months ago, as you no doubt recall.

But to return to my story, back in May we had just put the union troops to rout at Chancellorsville and I guess General Lee was feeling pretty full of himself. The way they explained it to us troops was that the General and his staff decided to take the war out of Virginia and let the Northerners get a taste of it for a change. They figured a major victory on northern soil might take a little starch out of the enemy. Plus, we were going to glean supplies as we crossed the Pennsylvania farmland - and we surely could use them.

Our party kept getting bigger and bigger as we marched north and kept joining up with other units. By the time we got to the outskirts of Gettysburg word was that we had a force of near 70,000 troops. Can you imagine? I'd wake up in the morning and step out of the tent (on those rare nights when we actually slept in a tent) and all I could see was an ocean of grey uniforms in every direction. They said it took a whole day for our entire column to march through a town, we had so many soldiers. That made me feel pretty good too, I'll say. It was hard to imagine anybody that could stand up to a fighting force like the Army of Northern Virginia. Of course, that was before we learned that the other side had deployed nearly 90,000 troops throughout the hills and ridges south of Gettysburg. I don't suppose even General Lee knew that before the battle.

Anyway, the fighting commenced on July 1st when we ran up on the Union forces west of Gettysburg. They had us stopped for a while until our reinforcements arrived and we pushed them back through the town and out into the hills. One of them was named 'Cemetery Hill' which was a very good name for what went on there. One of my good friends, Jessie Merchant, was killed there. His real name was Johnson, but his dad was a merchant so we called him Merchant. I guess if his dad had run a mill we'd have called him Miller. That was just our sort of joke. Jessie was a good friend, but he just wouldn't listen. We were under a barrage of cannon fire and our officers told us to hug the dirt and just keep crawling forward, but Jessie, for some reason, he had to stand up and holler at those boys in blue and when he did he caught a bullet right in his forehead. I wish Jessie was still here. I could have used a friend here in the hospital.

On the second day, General Lee had us moving around the Union flank. I recall walking through a place where the Union troops had tied up a bunch of horses to a fence. A shell had gone off right near the fence and there were dead horses everywhere. I thought that was real sad, 'cause you know how I like horses. Our side pushed 'em back again that day, but at great cost. And by sundown they still held strong positions along the front.

At one o'clock on the third day, July 3rd, General Lee ordered an all-out attack on the center of the Union line. Our division, headed by Major General George E. Pickett, led the charge. Our batteries sent up a huge barrage to soften the Union resistance, but we found out later that our cannons were shooting too high and most of the shot fell behind the Union lines and hardly helped us a bit. When we advanced to where the Union troops should have been in disarray, we found ourselves looking at rank after rank of riflemen, division after division of infantry. In the rear, they even had a regiment of cavalry waiting to shoot down any craven who fled from their post. They had out-thought us and out-manned us at every turn.

It was on that third day that I myself was hit. The surgeon who operated on me told me I had been hit by a Minié Ball, a new kind of bullet that the Union had, but we didn't. The Minié Ball is made of a soft lead that spreads when it hits something—shattering bones and tearing flesh. The one that hit me went through both thighs, just below the hips and the surgeon said there was nothing he could do, but to take both legs. I know that sounds horrible, but at least I'm alive, although not alive and kicking. (Ha Ha.) I know you hate to hear this, Ma, but truth is I feel fortunate seeing as how many men died here at Gettysburg.

One of our officers, Captain Ritter, came by the hospital a little while ago talking to me about how the whole of the Confederacy appreciated my sacrifice. It was a nice little speech and I bet he even meant it the first fifty or so times he gave it. But there were 51,000 men died here at Gettysburg and who knows how many injured? Captain Ritter didn't talk to all the injured of course, but I bet he'd given that speech way over a hundred times before he got to me. It surely sounded like it.

Anyway, Ma and Pap, your boy made it through. They told me I was going to be shipped out soon and would be on my way home, but God knows how long it'll take me to arrive. On the other hand, I might get there before this letter. Sorry I won't be able to help in the fields anymore, Pap. I guess I'll just have to help Ma peel spuds and shuck corn from now on.

I can't wait to see you both again.

Your loving son,
Hiram H. Milsap, Corporal,
14th Virginia
Army of Northern Virginia

& &

Muriel J. Muex

Count Your Blessings

The earth yields no crops,
and the children are starving;
a man's life is spent working;
he works 'til life stops.

An abusive husband,
viciously beats his wife.
Depression has caused another
to take his own life.

A family's belongings
are cast out on the street.
A homeless man
has no shoes on his feet.

An old woman lies alone
frozen in death.
A little girl fighting disease
gasps out her last breath.

The runaway teen on the street sells her wares,
hopelessly living a life of despair.
Another shoots dope,
having long since lost hope,
sadly believing that nobody cares.

Tornadoes, volcanoes, floods,
and slides of mud,
all take their due.
They twist and rage, and surge and spew.
Earthquakes, hurricanes, and other natural disasters;
man is powerless against mother nature.
Nothing can stop her except the Creator.

So, pray for those who have lost faith and hope,
pray for those who simply can't cope,
and when something for you is unduly stressing,
just think of those people and

Count Your Blessings!

1

Rhythm of Life

A couple face parenthood together,
While yet another
Vow to love and cherish forever.
That's the Rhythm of Life

The lustful protest of a baby's cry
as it emerges from the womb,
while the smell of lye
permeates the room.
That's the Rhythm of Life

The coming of Spring
turns the earth's coat green,
and melts the mountain snow
feeding the valley streams below.
That's the Rhythm of Life

The squeals of laughter
of the children at play
bring a smile to the weary mother
at the end of a grueling day.
That's the Rhythm of Life

Listening to the summer wind
as it whispers through the trees,
watching as they slowly sway
to the gently cooling breeze.
That's the Rhythm of Life

Watching the golden leaves
as they slowly turn brown,
and wither and shrink
and tumble to the ground.
That's the Rhythm of Life

Tears of loss flow freely
at the reciting of the eulogy
as the hard-packed earth is turned
and our loved one is buried deep.
That's the Rhythm of Life

Musings of the Soul

Hear the endless murmuring
of a spirit to be free.
Tightly bound in chains of doubt –
Are they cognizant of me?

Pulsing, rippling waves of force
lapping at my feet.
Fear and angst devour the Soul
'til the life-force becomes deplete.

One day I fear I shall withdraw
And withdrawing disappear,
like Atlantis on the ocean's floor,
existing nevermore.

With a dose of paregoric
Release the pain in me –
Give to me an anodyne
that I may clearly see.

Delve deep into your consciousness,
seek your own true bliss –
search for that which binds us all,
then you will hear the call.

Rise Up! Rise Up!
Essence core,
rise up and fill your cup,
to overflow with boundless wonders,
that lie through Zion's door.

What is Success?

Being the youngest in the family, I always had to go to bed earlier than anyone else, and it was a constant sore spot with me. My strategy was to wear my parents down by constantly asking and it worked, tonight I had success at last. I finally persuaded my parents to let me stay up to watch one more movie.

Filled with delight at my success, I ran up the stairs to quickly change into my pajamas. As small as I was, it was no small feat to take the stairs two at a time but tonight, I felt I could do anything. Unfortunately, in my haste, I forgot to turn on the hall light upstairs.

My euphoria propelled me to within a few steps of the top of the stairs. I reached that plateau of utter darkness, where unspeakable, horrible things lurked just beyond human sight, and I came to an abrupt halt. Caution took over as I stood staring, wide-eyed, at two gaping holes of darkness, one on my left, and the other on my right. Even as I told myself they were only the doorways to my parents' and sisters' bedrooms, I began to tremble and my legs became weak. It seemed logic had no place in this alien world of darkness.

Realizing I could not stand here forever, I took a deep breath. Very softly I started saying "there is really nothing there," as though it were a litany. I inched my way past the well of darkness toward my bedroom on the left, never once taking my eyes off the yawning maw of hell, which was the doorway to my parents' bedroom. Everyone knows that any sudden movement is an act of aggression. The denizens of the nether world would react to your presence and pounce on you before you could get past them. I very slowly moved along, my heart pounding against my chest, afraid that at any moment they would see me and my next move would be my last.

At last I reached the safety of my bedroom and I immediately flicked the light switch on. I expelled a long sigh of relief as light flooded the room. I started to close the door but thought better of it. The evil spirits that lurk in dark places surely knew of my presence. If I closed my door, it would shut out the light from my room. Without the light to protect me, I knew they could gather in droves outside my door and trap me in my room.

Looking out from the safety of my room, I checked the two, bedroom doorways. Discerning no movement and sensing no evil spirits, I deemed it safe to change into my night clothes. Turning, but still trying to watch the door, a necessary precaution, I bent to grab my pajama top from the bed. With a swiftness goaded by fear, I lifted the top over my head. I turned with my arms still extended over my head, and froze. In the doorway of my parents' bedroom, holding on to the doorframe, swinging back and forth while the other arm hung down by his side, was what I feared most, one of the denizens of the underworld.

I stood frozen in the act of putting on my top, too afraid to move, too afraid to look away, even too afraid to blink, as we stared at one another. Big, black, unblinking eyes watched me from the bedroom doorway as he slowly swung back and forth, back and forth. He was not quite the nightmare I expected, but he was surely strange looking.

Straight, coal-black hair hung down his face, nearly covering his large round eyes. One side of him was blue, skin and clothes, the other side was pink. What I found most alarming was the fact that he was dressed in the same kind of pajamas that I was about to put on. It made me think that he might be a changeling sent to replace me, but had not quite finished the change. My arms started to ache and still we stared at one another. I wondered why he just stood there; why didn't he make a move to grab me? Could it be the light keeping him at bay?

I uttered a brief prayer that he would go away, and strength immediately flowed through me. Anger slowly replaced my fear. Anger that he had the power to make me afraid. Anger that I let him control me through my fear. Anger that I was too afraid to move even though my arms hurt. Anger that he might be enjoying my fear. I couldn't take it anymore; whatever the outcome, I was going to make a move. Moving as quickly as I could, I thrust my arms through the sleeves of my pajamas and yanked the top over my head. When I looked again he was gone.

Was he really gone, or was he only hiding? I finished putting on my pajamas, never taking my eyes off the doorway, not daring to leave my room until I was sure he was truly gone. I stared into the empty darkness unsure of what to do next. For several minutes, that felt more like hours, I debated the issue. Finally, disgusted with myself, and impatient to get downstairs and see the movie, I dashed out of my room. I flicked the light switch off as I ran out and raced down the stairs, nearly falling in my haste to put some distance between me and the pink and blue boy and get downstairs where it was safe.

At the bottom of the stairs I looked back, half expecting to see him staring at me but saw nothing. Breathing a sigh of relief, I silently congratulated myself on successfully eluding a fate worse than death. My heart was still beating wildly when I slowly walked into the living room. My mother asked me what was wrong; why did I run down the stairs as if the demons of hell were after me. I went over to her and breathlessly related everything that had happened.

When I finished telling my story, I thought for sure she would soothe me, and tell me how brave and smart I was to escape the things that go bump in the night. I was totally disappointed and hurt when her only comment to my close brush with death was, "this is the last time you stay up this late." As I sat dejectedly on the floor with everyone's laughter ringing in my ears, I thought, "so much for my success."

Valeri Paxton-Steele

we are

you are the whirlwind voice on the mountain
and I the cascading echo of you
you are the inertia of the undying wind
ever flowing, moving, expanding
and I am the field of grass bending and swaying
dancing to you in my lazy way
we separately are the movements of the earth
the single bird in a flock of starlings
a snowflake riding air currents in a squall
but together we capture all the essence
of the gravity of binary stars
keeping track of each shifting motion
gravity attracting each body to body
interacting in our great "we are…"
each energy dependent on the other
influenced, elegant, simple in our complexity
we are our own coded patterns
imprinting ourselves on one another

yellow wallpaper

bedroom terror
sky darkens
rain patters
psychosis laughing
wailing wailing
goes unnoticed
precise patterns
intricately unusual
jumbles spins
scuttles slinks
dances creeps
scratching behind
yellow wallpaper
breaking down
stealthily slouching
crouching on
haunched knees
circling turning
around around
shouts echo
wall cracks
comes undone
wriggling struggling
writhing out
from between
laced latticework
embossed on
yellow wallpaper

peeling peeling
hinges creak
door opens
perfect escape
lunatic prisoner
madness unleashed
defying existence
long last
the freedom
claws skulks
loosed from
yellow wallpaper

a witch's blood

damned this girl
guards sent word
hail the townsfolk
long awaited months
crackle hooves beat
door squeaks open
shackles clank clang
gasping greed cowers
on weeping knees
unseen clouds pass
wind howls cold
hemorrhage spatters splashes
agony chants grunts
cold irons bite
ankle and wrist
bound hands tremble
wet nurse quiet
strikes distorted wailing
witch's baby cries
wrapped innocent coos
savage tears weep
vicious footsteps approach
prepare her killing
their influence succeeds
crowd assembles now
found guilty begs
belladonna hemlock henbane
strong drink thrust

terrified lips thirst
for haunted release
surrender to deathbed
captors leading captive
command and commanded
swooning feet float
light her will
iron inside her
iron chains bound
harsh approach undeserved
a fitting punishment
light hearted teen
horse bells jingle
last sound heard
ripping of flesh
disemboweled she lay
a witch's death
drawn and quartered
all transgressions annulled
pieces slipping away
the slaughter complete
wolves bear witness
grassy bones left
hard days over
blood on ferns
blood on ferns

The Lottery

Only the crops mattered.
This year the drought had taken hold.
Without the lottery,
their corn would fail to thrive.
The harvest was due reaping in
the next few months.
"It's Tessie," the crowd said.
Rocks in all shapes
and sizes were piled high.
Pebbles for the children
so they could feel their part
was done so justly.
The heavy ones plucked up
by those women who knew what
the word "mercy" meant.
Tessie said "It's not right."
Dust devils whirled around her feet.
She looked into the faces
of her friends, her neighbors.
Her eyes welled with tears.
The stones flew fast and hard.
"It's not ri-," her words cut off
as the thick stone hit her temple.
The crowd from the village
swarmed toward their sacrifice,
to this summer's latest offering,
rocks fisted in hand after steady hand.

The rain would come.
The corn would grow tall,
much taller than Tessie.

Tyne's Lyttle Task

My name is Isaac Tyne. I deal in ghosts, ghouls and things that go bump in the night. "Save me," she said, "from this world." I could not. No one could. There is no cure for her ills, not anymore. There is no cure for death. Her voice was like a bell, a small stunning harmonic tone echoing softly after each word she spoke inside my brain.

She seeped into my consciousness, weeping her fate.

"Purple Smoke" was fixing to have herself a seat at my kitchen table. It was no natural color that I have ever seen before. The closer she came, the more I wanted to let go of the last four cups of coffee I had guzzled down earlier.

The effect had me squirming in my seat much more than I wanted to.

Reaching out to spirits is decidedly dangerous. Now, ghosties with nasty grudges I have been through before, but this kind of sorrow left me clueless. You think I would have learned my lesson by now. The exception this time was the lack of vengeance. No malice in her spirit whatsoever.

From what I could tell, all the research said that she has been around for at least the last couple-few centuries. Here was a ghost who has haunted early America from practically its founding. She fascinated me.

I laughed. "Listen, Violet, or whatever your name is, no one can un-dead you!" Her shoulders visibly sagged, leaving little bits of purple aura smoke floating there in the air for a moment. Something about her just seemed so innocent, but I knew she couldn't have been. Spirits who hang around such as this one had, trying to communicate, scaring the hell out of people, almost never have pristine and untainted souls.

Her voice resonated, reverberated. "I accept that I am dead. I do not accept my burial. I cannot keep going on like this." Her sobbing leaked into my brain and settled heavily in my gut. I could feel every ounce of her pain. "Every day is the same. I'm trapped here forever. You have to help me."

I felt so sorry for her, this petite little thing. I almost wanted to reach out, to cup her hand in mine, to try to be some sort of comfort to her. The vague outline was hard to see, but she was there, sure enough. No mistaking it. A young woman. I couldn't really say how old, or what she looked like, but she was a woman. Of this much I was sure. I didn't need any damned newspaper articles to feel it, either.

When Ned Anderson's old Sunoco opened up, the stories started flying. His place was up near Five Mile Creek, about two miles from the center of town, up where the new interstate off-ramp was being built.

People started talking to each other about the strange things that happened around the spot where they passed Ned's. At first there were casual comments made at the supper table in between passing the potatoes and the gravy—"Hey, hon, I got the weirdest feeling as I was driving home today. I felt this headache, like a little foggy, you know? And I started seeing this purple smoke. I thought I was hallucinating or something. Then it passed, just as soon as it came on. Craziest feeling I've ever had. It scared me outta my wits. I thought I was having a stroke or something" Even Ned himself will tell you a story or two, if you've got the time to stay and jaw with him a bit.

After a while, with gossip being what it is, people started to put it together that a certain spot of old Route 11 was haunted. Fast forward through a couple of decades, and there it was in the tabloids, in all its glory. That's how I found her. Newspaper clippings dubbed her "The Violet Ghost." Just a foolish bit of deadly history hanging on by her fingernails to a life she could never touch again. In the ghost's presence, I could feel the centuries pass. Centuries she must have been waiting, hoping for peace.

Purple vapors wafted around her form. The silhouette behind the haze was terrified. The fear was contagious. It seemed that every emotion of hers also belonged to me. I had never sensed so much raw desperation before. Then she touched me.

"You have to find me. Please? I am underneath the creek bed. They sealed me in a stone coffin. They called me a witch. The top jolted open and now the water swirls all around me. It flows over my face. It burrows into my bones. The fish nibble and feed on me. It is impossible to break free. I do not belong there. I belong in hallowed ground—in the consecrated ground of the church."

I didn't know how, but I was gonna help her. There were so many unanswered questions. I felt her fear as they came for her. They bound her hands, and dragged her down to the water. The men from the village must have sweat buckets to get that damned box in the creek. High and mighty Puritans. Was this little slip of a girl so evil that they huffed and puffed that thing over acres of fields and hills? Why?

She screamed when they forced her in. Everyone heard the screaming, the distressed wailing, but no one stopped it. Her words became unintelligible—an incoherent string of babbling—pleading for mercy though her tears. She writhed and thrashed against the angry men. To the onlookers, it was more apparent than ever that there was evil inside her. The knees of her dress were stained with grass and mud. There was no escape from their rough hands as they forced her into the coffin. Her body disappeared under the weight of the heavy grey stone. The last man pulled his hand out quickly as his holy neighbors forced the lid into place.

Her name was Constance Lyttle. She had been out picking violets. She was a lot of things: disobedient, contentious, headstrong. She was also quite lovely, on the cusp of a glorious womanhood. It is said that "The Devil deals in discord," and she had rather gone hiding in the upper meadows than doing chores of carding cotton or shelling corn with her sisters. Once the murmurings against her started, the gossip-mongers won. She hadn't stood a chance against them. "Witch," they whispered. She showed me every moment of the terror as it unfolded.

Eerie wisps of her crazy electric violet color shuddered in front of me. It seemed like her senses got all mixed-up and went haywire at the last second. She wasn't a cloud, or an outline, or anything else substantial that I could put a name to, but I felt more in tune with her than with any other entity I have ever dealt with. I have been given the task. I realized then that I would never stop looking for her hellish underwater tomb. Her body is still out there, up in Five Mile Creek. No, I wouldn't stop, not until her innocent bones are buried in consecrated ground. Not until Constance Lyttle is lain to rest, and her soul finally finds some peace.

I took a walk down to the river basin, coursing my way slowly along the bank of 5 Mile Creek. The morning was overcast and damp. The grey sky was low and cloying. It seemed close enough to touch. The air was stagnant. It felt like heavy lead in my lungs. I knew my destiny was written in the soft mouldering leaves beneath my feet.

Where was she? I kept my eyes on the river, looking for the darkest, deepest green-black spots where her coffin could be concealed. She was lost, and only I could find her. Only I could save her. We had a connection. This trip was all about hunger. There was a hunger in her, lean and sharp, desperate to be found. There was a hunger in me, too, just as keen, longing to find her. I was a man possessed.

I began to glimpse visions of hell. The hell of being snatched away from my family—the hell of being dragged through fields of flowers. Violets. Dragged through violets on a carpet of sweet, green, summer grass. The smell filled my nostrils, then my mouth. I could taste the green and the purple and the dirt. I knew I was getting closer to her tomb. The terror rose in my throat. I looked left, just as the turn in the river started to bend. It was there. The moss grew thick on the river stones. Wintergreen grew in wild clumps among the woodland cover. Her terrible resting place was sheltered by a thick stand of maple and birch trees. And just there, vibrant among the rest, on this grey day, a cluster of violets. I tasted mud. Mud and blood. I waded out, into the creek.

The coffin's lid was askew. The burial depth was so great that I could only see a sick blackness within it, but the current allowed me great strength—strength enough to move the solid stone slab away from the box. I reached down, my body shivering with a sudden gust of wind, or spirit, or god knows what. I touched the rounded form of a centuries old skull. Was that her hair I felt, or just the ghost of it? Maybe it was long overgrown algae. I don't really know. What I do know is that there was a lightness, like the lifting of a heavy weight, as I pulled her up from that brown swirling sarcophagus. I uncovered the body of that poor, sweet teenage girl. I found the sad remains Constance Lyttle. And I intend to bring her home.

ß ß

Carole Kays Schaefer

A Heart of Gold

It had been a long day for Lucy, but before she clocked out, she'd check on Miss Caroline. As was her routine for the last four years, she made sure her favorite ward had fresh water and a bit of TLC. "Miss Caroline, it's end of shift. How about some fresh water?" Lucy asked as she pushed the control which raised the bed's head.

"Lucy, dear girl, You're so good to me. You remind me of a doll my mother gave me—unpretentious in appearance, but with a heart of gold." Lucy thought the old lady's comment was odd, but sweet.

"Today is Emma's birthday. I've made an angel food cake with her favorite icing, princess pink, of course, and there is a piece saved for you." The old lady's eyes brightened.

Back at her locker, Lucy zipped her thinning parka, and mentally organized her route home—first stop, the thrift shop where the Barbie doll, still in its original box, was on hold for her; then on to the supermarket for ice cream and candles; last stop, afterschool care for her sweet Emma.

As she scurried past the Golden Years Retirement Center sign to the parking lot, she prayed her old Toyota would start in this January deep freeze—her conscience implored—*where was that child support check, David had promised?*

That night Lucy's mom, Mary, and her sister, Irene, came over making it a real birthday party. Thank God for family. *Damn her useless, irresponsible ex. He hadn't called or even sent a card.* Mercifully, Emma, only five, distracted by the celebration, seemed unaffected by his absence.

Next morning, rushing through all her single-parent duties, Lucy just made it in time to hear the night shift report. She noted the usual happenings—until the words, "Last night we lost Miss Caroline." Those unexpected words cut deeply, cracking her usual hardened acceptance of death. In self-defense, she dropped her head, and muffled a sob.

Lucy made it through the day, tending her charges and clearing out Miss Caroline's room. The sum of her possessions barely filled a cardboard box. One item, a yellowing photograph of a winsome young woman, in a white sailor tunic, holding hands with a tall, rail-thin, young man, brought consolation, a heartening reminder that Miss Caroline had enjoyed a long and loving marriage as Mrs. John Lodge.

A few nights later near bedtime, Lucy's phone rang. Hesitant to answer, she noticed it was a local number, not likely a debt collector, so she picked up. A business-like voice, asked, "Is this Mrs. Lucy St. John?"

"Yes?"

"Mrs. St. John, sorry to call so late, but I have tried numerous times today. I am Simon Welch, attorney, and I represent the late Caroline Lodge estate. Mrs. Lodge has bequeathed an item to you."

Lucy's heartbeat quickened. "Repeat that please."

"Now Mrs. St. John, there is no great value to this bequest, I suspect; but Mrs. Lodge specifically wanted you to have it. It's a wooden trunk she kept in storage. I can have it delivered at your convenience."

The inheritance arrived the next day, just an antique, old, dome-topped trunk. Its contents were as expected, mementos of a lifetime—a packet of old post cards, three dried corsages, a flat-crowned, navy, felt hat, a pile of vintage clothes, and a raggedy cloth doll. *What, this is an inheritance?* Lucy thought. But Emma saw it as a pirate's treasure, especially the old doll. She cuddled it in her arms, as she whirled around the room, declaring that thereafter it would be Caroline Ann because, "she looks like Raggedy Ann."

Later that evening, Emma came into the kitchen crying. "Mommy, Mommy, Caroline Ann is hurt. She has a hole in her back."

Lucy expected the fragile, old, cloth body had split due to the child's exuberant handling. But a quick inspection proved that not to be. Instead there were only broken threads of a hand-stitched seam.

Dr. Mom to the rescue. Lucy gathered a needle and thread and began stitching. "Darn, the needle's hit something hard."

That something lodged between the doll's shoulders proved to be a small burnished gold coin.

How odd, she thought as she eased it out, *probably one of Caroline's childhood "treasures."* Holding that thought, she completed the repair and stashed the coin in her own "treasure" jewelry box.

Lucy's Saturdays were fully scheduled. Today she planned a stop at the pawn shop to reclaim her Seiko—and acting on a whim, she decided to take Caroline's old coin for appraisal. But first was their weekly visit to the library. While Emma enjoyed story time, Lucy took advantage of the free computers.

Finding an open place at the work station, she waited as the computer booted up. The screen flashed—I'm Feeling Lucky—that prompted her. She decided to Google "coins." Up popped a gallery of rare coin pictures. There among them was a coin, called a Brasher doubloon, almost identical to Caroline's "treasure." Lucy's mind began to fire with possibilities.

She scanned the computer information further...*dates to George Washington's time...only seven struck, but only six exist today... hallmarked EB... valued between $500,000 and $2,500,000 dollars.*

Lucy's hands shook as she pulled the coin from her bag. She turned it over. There on the eagle's wing were the letters EB! "Oh, my God," she cried, raising eyebrows among those in earshot. What to do?

She called her sister Irene, her closest confidant, and the most cool-headed family member. In addition, Irene was a lawyer's secretary, with access to free legal advice. Irene was at Mom's today doing her laundry.

"Sis, I need some help, meet me at the library NOW?"

"What, I'm up to my bum in dirty laundry, can't it wait?" Irene said.

"I mean it Sis, I need you NOW!"

Lucy met the ill-tempered Irene at the library entrance, but with Lucy's news, Irene quickly warmed. The two continued searching the internet. Every click revealed another point of coin verification.

Irene knew their next move. She directed Lucy to Wechsler Auction House, a renowned national rare coin dealer.

Monday, Lucy made the call. The stars must have been aligned just right, for the expert she spoke to would be in her area soon, doing an Antique Roadshow. From Lucy's description of the coin, he agreed to meet with her on show day, before the doors opened to the public.

Fortunately for the sisters, the show fell on a Saturday, their day off. With restrained hope and an early start, the sisters traveled downtown to Municipal Auditorium. They parked in the underground garage, took the elevator up to third floor and followed arrows leading to a door marked, Business Office. A harried receptionist, juggling incoming calls, questioned and aimed them down the hall.

The sisters entered a large conference room. There near the coffee station, cup in hand, stood Mr. Winston, a silver-haired gentleman, perfectly groomed. Suddenly the absurdity of the moment hit the two. They froze; but within seconds, Irene found her voice.

Mr. Winston, apparently, was a very busy fellow, with no time for amenities, not even a handshake. They moved to the conference table where he pulled from his briefcase, a pair of white cotton gloves. Meekly Lucy handed over the coin. He took it in hand, reached for his magnifying glass and scrutinized each section of its surface. His pale face reddened. Then he took a deep breath and said, "I can't say with certainty, but from my vast experience, (modesty not among his virtues) this does appear to be a Brasher doubloon. Though only our forensic specialists can determine its absolute authenticity."

Time and space became surreal. Irene guided Lucy to a chair.

Breaking character, a more amiable, more respectful Mr. Winston addressed the sisters, "Dear ladies, (another deep breath) "This is extraordinary (displaying the coin in his palm)!" "Collectors have dreamed this seventh doubloon would surface for over 150 years, but most believed that the coin was lost when the family who owned it were lost at sea. It was assumed the coin was at the bottom of the Atlantic. How did it come into your possession?"

Lucy still in a dreamlike state, regained sense enough to answer, "I inherited it from a wonderful friend," and she added, "who had a heart of gold."

℞ ℞

Mary Silwance

Treat Yourself

My mother
presses a twenty into my hand.
Breathless with housebroken passion
she whispers

                              get a manicure
then steps back smiling, smug
like it was a vibrator
she just handed me   known to do the job well
solve my problems
make everything better
make my dreams come true
flatten my belly
remove cellulite
stop me from feeling so other all the damn time.

Later, I spent the twenty
on black pants that promised to
solve my problems
make everything better
make my dreams come true.

But when I got home
the pants contracted
all the dimples in my ass showed
my belly bulged like a bowling ball.
So, I spent another twenty on scotch,
got a buzz.
Everything was better.

It did the job well.

Home Sweet Home

Vacant boxes stack the closet
brittle rubber bands
trap moldy memories
desk-drawers graveyard
spent batteries and unknown keys
calcified condiments
congest the fridge
neglected repairs ghost the basement
dust flurries books
shelved with uncracked spines.

rooms
full
of

      nothing.

(Untitled)

bitter is a bird

slender foot
tethered to
a long lead.

Roams far
not free.

Returns
instead

ravenous

for
heart meat
still
pulsing.

ଌ ଓ

Irene Sims

I Wonder

I wonder what happened to
Good old common sense?
Where has gone old fashioned decency?
Respect, honor, gentility, niceties
All seem gone.

As an American, how do we appear to others?
Think of the consequences
Do we care?
I wonder.

Founded
On such a wonderful history
Of a country created for its people
For the rules of law
The foundation, a caring for all.
Ability to love, learn, and grow
Peacefully, gracefully, and hopefully.
Have these values disappeared?

I wonder and I fear.
Foundation of a nation—education
Education to prepare us for life
To earn a living, develop relationships,
Enjoy daily living.
Grow and develop satisfaction in life

Make good decisions
Love self, others, beauty, and everyday living.

Always learning and serving
Maturing in a complicated world
With integrity, with considerations for others
A respect for true beauty of all things
Around us
For different culture, for our environment
And the betterment of our universe.

Rex the Hex or Scoop the Poop

Rex the hex is he for hire?
Just discovered you got poop on the wire!

Dogs need dipping, they got lice
NO TIME! Poop on the wire, he told you twice.

Puppies need vaccinations and also worming
NO TIME! Rex has you squirming.

Poop on the wire! Poop on the wire!
Rex says he can't stand the mire.

Just let other things wait and wait.
Rex is knocking at the gate.

You know what will be his theme
Poop on the wire, a bad, bad dream.

Sometimes you wonder what he's at
At the computer, he sat and sat.

He writes and writes and forward leans
But poop on the wire is what he means.

Rex the hex, is he for hire?
Cause all he thinks is, POOP ON THE WIRE!

The Eighties

Eyes that can't see well
Ears that don't hear tell

Of an older age
Oh, turn a fear-filled page.

Not only is our hair thin
Other problems now begin.

Pain—here and there
Begins to be our care.

My legs, my back, my gear
Are stiffer and slower each year.

My gait has become so slow
My strength weak and low.

Days seem longer and longer
Nights have become a gonger.

Oh goodness, at a cry
To get better, we try and try

Each day we do our best
But fail to pass the test

Given for us to survive
No longer perfection to arrive.

But it seems very clear
The end may be near.

But I go on and hope and hope
To be able my way to grope.

Now for today I will be
Happy for tomorrow, glad to see.

ଔ ଓ

Billie Holladay Skelley

Static Electricity

It is always the same
on this board game of life,
short periods of happiness
intermingled with larger ones of strife.

As a couple committed to repeated moves
in a game known simply as husband and wife,
they've become warriors armed only with
a scabbard of insults that cut deep as a knife.

He strays,
then lies.
She accuses.
He denies.

Traveling across their daily playing board,
in moves calculated to resemble living,
they've become hollow, manipulated pieces
driven by a taking strategy that forbids giving.

Checkmated before the next move begins,
they've never fought on the same side.
They constantly embrace the battle,
but remain unable to stem the tide.

She strays,
then lies.
He accuses.
She denies.

Their fighting achieves nothing,
except sparks of heat and flashes of light,
not enough to warm or illuminate,
just sufficient to sting and further incite.

Control

The waves waltz
Successively
Across the sandy dance floor
Pounding with a rhythm
My body cannot ignore.
I see, hear, and feel them
Washing
Away the world
Engulfing
Me by degrees
Swallowing
All they touch
With each repetitive beat
Vanishing.
But wait...
I have to
Remember.
I did not select this song
Nor the dance steps being performed
It is out of my control
I cannot move the waves
I can only move me.

Waving in the Wind

Sunflowers stand proudly in the fields,
Turning their faces to the sky,
Looking to the sun for answers—
Radiating hope to all who pass by.

Straining for truth in each ray of light,
They dance in unison with the wind.
Golden petals fluttering in flight—
A message of promise they send.

Even when grey skies threaten,
To leak their lies all around,
These dancers stand firm and unafraid,
Waiting patiently for the sun to be found.

Lies cannot wash away the truth,
Any more than lightning can harm the sky.
Sunflowers just soak up the fortifying rain,
And wait for the dark clouds to pass by.

Sometimes to truly see the light,
Darkness must completely surround,
But if there is hope dancing in the air,
Truth and beauty can always be found.

Surviving Joplin's EF-5 Tornado

A normal afternoon in May suddenly transformed
by a twisting dragon hell-bent on destroying
everything in its reach.
For 32 minutes, it rears its ugly head blowing
powerful winds that
uproot trees and demolish homes.
Swooping down in destructive strikes without a care in
the world,
it viciously wields its power—
damaging or destroying eight thousand structures,
injuring more than a thousand people,
and taking more than one hundred and sixty lives.
Nothing is as it once was.
I no longer know where I am.
Shards of glass, pieces of wood, and twisted metal are all
that remain.
It is total devastation—an apocalyptic event.
The landscape is changed forever.
My heart is changed forever.
Devastation, hurt, and loss turn to grief and despair.
Life as I know it is over...
But right when you realize your world is gone,
you somehow reach inside
and find courage you didn't know you had.
You discover it in the strangest places—
in your own muscles, in a neighbor's smile,
in a friend's hug, and in a stranger's helping hand.
You see it in a butterfly drinking nectar
from the last flower left on the block.
You think to yourself: "If it can go on, so can I."
You make yourself get up each morning.

You remove debris, clean, and replace.
Eventually, signs of healing and hope return.
You feel stronger and improved for being tested
and for meeting the challenge.
Dragon memories fade as butterflies flourish.
Resilience and insight led to recovery.
You realize life is changed, but it is not over.
Things are gone, never to be replaced,
but you understand they are just things.
You discover what really matters in life—
It is compassion, caring, and love.

Marilyn K. Smith

An Army Brat

An Army brat, that was me. I went to six different grade schools and two high schools. I learned early on not to get close to anyone, because it hurts too much to be pulled away. Sure, I heard, "I'll write," but after a few months the letters stopped coming. Not to make friends in the first place was my best defense.

I guess the best friend I ever had was Jeremy Blancett. His mother was my fifth-grade teacher. She was the one who came to my rescue the afternoon I missed the bus.

On the Thursday before my first week of school, at Clarkston, Mom and I arrived at the huge brick schoolhouse. We walked through the double doors, and headed to the principal's office. The secretary, Marlene Pinkerton—I'll never forget her. She was short, round, had ruby red lips and enough rouge that her cheeks matched her lips, and a smile that would soothe anyone's fears. She filled out all the paperwork, and gave us the twenty-cent tour. The three-story school was old, with wooden floors that creaked beneath our feet, and stairways here, there and everywhere. Mrs. Pinkerton took us up one set of stairs, down a long hall, around a corner and in front of the room I would soon call my own. A cardboard cutout of a round, blue

balloon identified the classroom as being Mrs. Blancett's
5th grade.

Military housing was the worst, but that particular
move Dad rented a house about eight miles from the
base. He said he wanted us to have as normal a life as
possible. We had a big yard, lots of trees, faraway
neighbors, and quiet nights. Believe me apartment
living is not quiet and peaceful, on an Army base.

Mrs. Pinkerton said the bus would arrive around
7:15. I was among the first students on, so I expected a
lengthy ride and I got it. That first morning when we
arrived at school, everyone went running and I followed
behind. We went into a door I had never seen, and once
inside nothing looked the same. I was still standing
there when I heard a lady say, "Are you lost?"

"Yes, I guess so," I told her. "I'm looking for Mrs.
Blancett's room."

"Come on, I'll show you." She even took me into
Mrs. Blancett's room and introduced me. "This young
lady is a new student," then she looked over at me,
expecting me, I guess, to say my name.

"Rebecca Wilham, but I prefer to be called Becca."

"Welcome, Becca. Your seat will be right here," and
she pointed to the desk three spots back, next to the
windows.

First days were the worst, especially if I started mid-
year. The other students knew each other, and I was the
odd-girl-out. That first day at Clarkston went smoothly
though, and when the last bell rang I grabbed my jacket
and followed the others. I didn't want to get sidetracked,

because I might not find the door I came in that morning.

"Hey, you in the blue," I heard a boy say. I looked around, but saw no one wanting to talk to me. Then someone tapped me on the shoulder. "You dropped your jacket." I didn't drop my jacket, he jerked it out of my grasp.

"Thanks!" and I reached for the jacket, but he pulled it away.

"Here, take your jacket," he said. When I reached for it, he pulled it away again. All kinds of thoughts were swirling through my head, such as *I'd like to knock the pee out of this kid*, but I knew better than to show my anger.

Boy Army brats—I've often wondered if it was easier for boys? They can fight to get their frustrations out. We girls have to grin and bear it. "Hey, Blue, here's your jacket." *Should I even pursue this ridiculous game he was playing, or should I let the kid keep my jacket?* Letting him keep my jacket is what I chose. Realizing I wasn't going to fight back, he threw it over into the corner. Another kid picked it up and came running to give it to me.

Then it occurred to me I had no idea what bus I rode that morning; # 8, I wasn't sure. I definitely would recognize the driver, because he was a dark-skinned American Indian. As quickly as my legs would carry me, I ran from bus to bus looking for my driver. Before I could peer into all the buses, the first ones began to pull out. "No, wait! Wait!"

I hurried back to the school, and the boy who had grabbed my jacket, causing me to miss my bus, was standing there. Tears, by this time, were forming. "What's the matter, Blue, did you miss your bus?"

Not returning a word, I kept walking. When I saw Mrs. Blancett, I burst into tears. She put her arm around me and asked, "What's wrong?"

"I missed the bus."

"Okay, let's go to the office and we'll see what can be done."

Miss Pinkerton to the rescue. "Mrs. Blancett, this girl lives about a half mile from you. Do you think you could drop her off?"

"Sure. Meet me at the back door in 15 minutes."

A bathroom break and drink of water occupied the time, and when I reached the door, Mrs. Blancett and a young girl walked up, but so did that jacket-snatching idiot.

"Hi, Honey," Mrs. Blancett said while roughing up the boy's hair. "Ready to go?" We made another step or two, and she said, "Becca, meet my son, Jeremy and my daughter Danielle." I wanted to—oh how I wanted to—blurt out about her son's earlier behavior, but I figured I would make more points with her if I kept quiet.

With our seatbelts securely fastened, she took off. "So, you live near me. What street?"

"Prichard's Bend. We're the end house, up on top of that hill," I said while pointing to the highest hill anywhere around.

"Oh, yes, I'm familiar with that place. One of my students lived there a couple of years ago. Army, I guess?"

"Yes, Army."

"Most folks around here are. I'm not, but most folks are." Silence took over, then she said, "Jeremy, tell her about your new colt."

The way his mother's rearview mirror was angled, she could see our every move, so giving him the evil eye or punching him in the gut was not an option. I couldn't even ignore him, because Mrs. Blancett would wonder why? The new colt story dragged on and on. Their neighbor's mare gave birth to a colt, and they bought it for Jeremy, yada, yada, yada. "I'll take you by to see it," Mrs. Blancett said. "It is on our way."

The mare and colt were in the pasture near the road. Mrs. Blancett stopped so we could see them. I had never seen a baby horse before, and although I was quite impressed I didn't say a word. I didn't want to give Idiot Boy even one drop of attention.

At home that evening, Mom and Dad asked all about school? I filled them in on how I entered the school through a different door, and how a lady took me to Mrs. Blancett's room, and that I am way ahead of the rest of the students in my studies. I don't know why, but I didn't tell them about Idiot Boy.

The days passed uneventfully, and spring break finally arrived. Always in the past, Mom and I traveled to Memphis where her sister lived, then on to Kentucky where Grandpa and Grandma lived. But this time she and several of the Army wives were taking their children to an amusement park, an indoor water park and to a museum. We were to ride with Mrs. Kendrickson and her daughters. The Kendrickson girls weren't just Army brats, they were brats. I wasn't looking forward to spending three days with them.

The morning we were to leave, Mrs. Kendrickson called. One of her girls came down with strep throat and she had to cancel, but "you can ride with Mrs. Blancett," she said. "She and her two kids are taking our spot." *You've got to be kidding. Spend three days with Idiot Boy—closed up in a car with him. The Kendrickson girls would have been better.* Since Mrs. Blancett lived close, she would be picking us up, Mom said.

Luggage loaded, and everyone belted into place, the first leg of our trip began. Man was I glad Idiot Boy had a younger sister who sat between us. Mrs. Blancett punched buttons so that the radio played kid-friendly music through the rear speakers only, and I guess that was supposed to make us more content on our long, three-hour trip.

Danielle was nice, nothing like her older brother. I guess she took after her mother. I liked Mrs. Blancett. Idiot Boy must have inherited his father's traits.

We arrived at the amusement park about noon, and the moms handed out money so we kids could buy whatever we wanted to eat. Then we were turned loose to ride rides. As long as we stayed together and reported in every hour, we were free to venture from place to place the rest of the day.

I guess that afternoon was when Jeremy and I finally became friends. We were the only ones who liked the fast rides, so we pretty well had to pair up. We even rode the big rollercoaster two times, and the parachute drop three times. We would have gone on that ride even more if we hadn't run out of time. "Can we come back tomorrow," Jeremy asked his mother, but no we couldn't, they already had plans for the next day.

Summer vacation that year was fun. Jeremy and Danielle invited me to go horseback riding, bike riding, picnicking and to the movies. They had several friends they palled around with, so we never lacked for companions.

They even threw me a going away party that next May—a year and a half in one place—almost a record. The last morning before we moved, Jeremy, on his own without me asking, promised to write. We exchanged E-mail addresses, and to my surprise he kept his promise.

In the seven-and-a-half years we did correspond, I learned that he took my jacket because he was attracted to me. "That's the way boys do things," he said, "and I've never met another girl I thought I would enjoy stealing her jacket from as much as I enjoyed stealing yours."

I kept him abreast of our moves to Germany, Wisconsin, Nebraska and California. One of his last messages said he would visit me if I didn't live so far away. California is a bit of a drive, I told him.

In our exchanges, we poured out our innermost thoughts; first kisses, tough math tests, learning to drive, fender-benders, prom dates, horrible sore throats, being grounded, and good and bad teachers. We wrote about happy times and not-so-happy times. One of the happy times for me was when I met Clint, and how we had hit it off right from the start. He loved to ride the fast rides, and his grandfather had horses. Jeremy, too, met a girl he was fond of. Her name was Andrea. Then less than three months for me and five months for Jeremy, both of our hearts were broken.

Can a person fall in love through an almost daily E-mail correspondence? I believe they can. I guess we will see if those feelings carry through when we are together face-to-face? Dad and I are traveling back to Jeremy's neck of the woods, so I can scout out college possibilities. If a spark really isn't there, remaining best of friends will have to do.

ও ঙ

Writers Having Fun

৪০ ~ ০৪

Writers Having Fun

Writers like to have fun, and the members of Boonslick Creative Writers follow the norm.

I'm not even sure who brought in the prompt, but we thought it was just the thing for the lovely weather we were having.

If you have hesitated writing to prompts, this may give you a new outlook on what can happen.

Following are four of the works telling what might happen when you go

Camping in God's Country!
1.
Elizabeth Davis

It seems that everyone thinks somewhere else is always better than where they are. Growing up in the sticks is one such example. We had no pavement, no nearby houses, no stores ... well, you get the picture.

When I moved to Kansas City, it was a whole new world. We had everything, or so I thought.

Then a funny thing happened. All my co-workers, city slickers every last one of them, went on vacation to the lake, or camping, or on road trips in ... wait for it ... the sticks.

It was so strange. I had spent eighteen years trying to get out of the sticks only to encounter a world of people waiting fifty weeks to spend two weeks there.

When I finally got a vacation, as in a whole week at one time, I didn't have the money to "go" anywhere, so I went back home. I spent a whole uninterrupted week watching the sun rise over a green field of grazing cattle in the east and sink beneath rolling hills in the west. No pavement, no people, no noise. It was wonderful discovering I grew up in God's country and didn't have to wait fifty weeks to go camping.

2.
Liz Priesendorf

It's here, it's here, it's finally here!

VA-CA-TION!

I get off of work at 2:15 p.m. and fly back to Boonville from Columbia. My husband Buddy has the "list" and is supposed to have our items laid out and packed into the Blazer. Well, half right. He has items out and is flopped down watching TV waiting for me. I start to fuss. "What are you doing? Why don't you have anything packed?"

"Now you know as well as I do," he said, "that if I had everything packed, you would have taken it all out again so you could mark each item off the list so we didn't miss anything."

Darn it! I hate it when he's right, and I hate it more when he uses my own words and past actions against me!

So, we mark every item off the list, while we pack them in their appropriate boxes, bags, or compartments. I'm so excited!

We have been camping and canoeing with our next-door neighbor Chris for years, so we have a pretty good idea of our necessities versus our wants. (Both are important!)

Everything is finally checked, double-checked, and packed in the truck. We gas up and begin to wagon train across the state to the southeast Ozarks. We pull into Echo Bluff State Park, the newest in Missouri, and our camp ground at Timbuktu, site #43.

Quick—unpack, unload, set-up the tents. Set the firewood where it goes. Get the food coolers and drinks where they go. Everything is staked down and we're finally ready to relax!

We take a break, sit down, take a breath and... Oh my God! Thank you for this!

We are in a valley, kind of a bowl. We have beautiful tree-covered Ozark mountains surrounding us on all sides. Sinking Creek to the east and Current River to the south. The sky has scattered puffs of clouds mixed in pink and shades of orange topped with blue sky icing.

It doesn't matter if we "do" anything, or even move—this is amazing! God is truly great and wondrous.

This is Camping in God's Country.

Thank you, Lord!

3.
Linda Runnebaum

Camping in God's country, that was what my husband had suggested two nights ago. I knew what he meant by that statement—Kansas. Yes, Kansas. He grew up in northeast Kansas and called it "God's Country". But, camping? Seriously? I love my husband and I love Kansas. Well, sort of. But, camping? Where were we going to find a camping spot in Kansas? The view would be great, I'm sure. We'd be able to see for miles, no matter where we were. The state was as flat as a pancake. I'm sure he had a plan but I was a bit leery.

I sat quietly as the truck jostled down the back road. I looked out at the farmland lining the street. I hoped we weren't going to be backed up to a pasture or a corn field. I cringed.

"We're almost there," my husband said as we turned onto another dirt road.

"Where are we going anyway?"

"It's a surprise," my husband said, continuing to smile.

I sighed. Our boys were so lucky. They were camping, too. But, they had stayed over on the Missouri side and were camping with the boy scouts down at the Lake of the Ozarks. Lucky boys, I thought to myself.

"Here we are!" My husband turned the corner after a small group of trees and stopped the truck. I looked ahead, and I couldn't believe my eyes. I had to sit and let the view sink in.

There before me was the most beautiful picture of God's country I'd ever seen. Of course, I could have probably found the same beauty in Missouri but my husband had called in a favor from a friend. There before us was a log cabin sitting in front of a stream lined with wild flowers and a pasture full of...no, not beef cattle, but horses. Yes, horses. I counted them...Ten beautiful Arabian horses grazing in a field of bright green grass.

I looked over at my husband. "You do know me, don't you?"

He smiled, "Well, like I said, 'God's Country'. Even God likes horses."

4.
Judy Stock

We pulled into the camp grounds about two hours before sunset.

Bill and Bobby got the tent pitched and took off to catch supper.

Ginny helped me get things "sorta" sorted out.

We got the cots set up with sleeping bags on them. I know, a snake could get on a cot, too, but it makes me feel more in control.

The duffels were put on the appropriate cots.

I set up the "kitchen." That consisted of the small gas grill, the five-gallon water cooler, a cook table and our chairs.

Then I started in on chopping lettuce, slicing tomatoes, and cutting veggies and putting them on skewers.

Around about that time, Bill and Bobby came back with a couple of rainbows big enough to feed us well.

Bill cleaned the trout, while I got grease in the cast iron skillet and put it on the hot side of the grill to warm up.

We had a relaxing meal, and I cleaned up afterwards.

Bill had his guitar out playing quietly, then he sang a few Country/Western songs. Bobby, Ginny and I sang along.

We turned in early. It had been a bad drive through rain the early part of the day, and we were tired. The sun coming out later had cheered us up, but didn't make up for the physical challenge of driving through heavy rain.

All of us were asleep immediately.

I don't know how much later it was when we were awakened by a truck horn blasting and the camp manager yelling, "Get up! Get up! Pack fast and get the heck out of here. Move. The water's going to be coming up fast."

I didn't know it was possible to break camp so quickly. I can't say we paid much attention to how carefully we packed. We just threw it all in.

The next morning, we stood on the hill overlooking the camp ground, watching the roiling water washing brush it had gathered upstream across where all of us campers had our tents pitched the night before.

God's Country had changed to Satan's hangout in minutes.

Note: We wrote to the same prompt, but what we wrote ended up entirely different. We do hope you enjoyed being taken along on our vacations, when we went Camping in God's Country.

ဆ ဆ

Author Bios

Vicki Cox

Vicki Cox is author of eleven children's books for Chelse House and McGraw Hill, Rising Stars and Ozark Constellations, an anthology of people and places in the Ozarks, and five-hundred feature articles in such publications as Harris' Farmers' Almanac, Chicago Tribune, Christian Science Monitor, American Profile Magazine, Western Horseman and regional newspapers and magazines in 16 states. She is a retired educator in Missouri public schools and adjunct teacher for Drury University (Springfield, Missouri) and past president of Missouri Writers' Guild.

Anita Crews

Anita Crews was a retired business woman, a mother, grandmother and great grandmother. She quilted, crocheted and played the piano.
Anita wrote fiction; genres varied. *Toby's Antics* (children); *When Seconds Count, The House of Emerald Gray,* and *Today's Assault ~ Yesterday's Crime*. All are available in print and ebook. She was published in The Columbia Chapter of Missouri Writers' Guild's *Well Versed—Literary Works* for 2014 and for 2015. This was her first "attack" on a Sestina.

Elizabeth Davis

Elizabeth (Liz) Davis is a columnist, news writer, and photographer for the Boonville Daily News. She's won awards from the Missouri Writers' Guild, the Columbia Chapter of the Missouri Writers' Guild, and Rock Springs Review. Recently, she added book editing to her repertoire. Off the clock, she writes mysteries and romances. She's currently working on a nonfiction reference book about the United States Supreme Court. In her spare time, Liz loves to read, crochet, and spend time with family.

Gail Denham

Gail Denham, despite having a large family and many grandchildren, wrote and published many stories, news articles, poems, and photos over her thirty-six-years career. Her emphasis is often story and humor, plus family. Denham belongs to many state poetry associations and regularly wins at contests, often published online. Recent wins include a 2nd prize in Galaxy of Verse contest; publication in Peninsula Poets, Paw Prints in Verse (one of her photos used also), and publication in 2017 Poetry Challenge Pioneers & Prairie—this anthology also used her photo on the cover.

Jane Hale

Jane Shewmaker Hale resides on the Hale family farm in Buffalo, Missouri. She and her late husband, Bob, have four sons, ten grandchildren, and seven great-grandchildren. She is an active partner in family businesses. She is a charter member of Ozark Writer's, Inc., Missouri Writers' Guild, VP, 2003-04, President 2005-06 columnist, "Buffalo—As I Remember it" in *County Courier*, YA series of mysteries: *Wonderland* 1997, *Heartland* 1999, *Foreverland* 2001, and *Boomland*, 2003. *Every Day Is Mother's Day* 2003, *Every Day Is Father's Day* 2006. Numerous short stories in Anthologies.

Diane L. Kehres

Diane L. Kehres earned a Bachelors in Nursing (BSN) from the University of Kansas, and spent thirty-plus years in the field of professional nursing. For the past two years, she has devoted her time to writing fiction. She is a contributor to the recently published "Winter 2016 Writers Bloc Anthology". She attended the Iowa Summer Writing Festival in 2016, and enjoys associations with The Writers Place (Kansas City, Missouri) Critique Group, The Writers Bloc, The Missouri Writers Guild, Kansas-Missouri Chapter of Sisters in Crime. Her work includes three novels, a series of short stories, poetry, and short fictional works.

Marilyn Hope Lake

Marilyn Hope Lake, Ph.D., writes short fiction, poetry, plays, and children's picture books. She is known widely for her children's book, *Buddy and the Grandcats*, published in 2007, which has sold over 500 copies, and is now available in a 2nd edition titled *Two Cats and A Dog*. She has been published in *Rock Springs Review, Stir, Well-Versed,* and the *Mizzou Alumni Magazine*. Her love of life, family, friends, nature and God is seen in her work. Lake travels between Kansas and Missouri to be with beloved family and canine companions.

Frank Montagnino

Frank Montagnino is a retired advertising man who has had hundreds of pieces published—in the form of ads, brochures, etc. Blown out of New Orleans by Hurricane Katrina, he landed in Columbia, where he fell in with the scoundrels in the Columbia Chapter of the Missouri Writers' Guild. There he discovered that like golf, his other passion, writing will drive you crazy. Although a few novella-length pieces have escaped his computer, he stays mainly with short stories, because frankly, he doesn't have anything to say.

Muriel J. Muex

Muriel is from St. Louis, Missouri, and is retired from Laclede Gas Co., where she worked as an Executive Assistant. She holds a BA in Organizational Studies from St. Louis University's School for Professional Studies and an MA in Speech Communication from Southern Illinois University in Edwardsville. She teaches part-time at Florissant Valley Community College and St. Louis University. In her spare time, she reads, crochets, and writes; not necessarily in that order.

Valeri Kathleen Paxton-Steele

Binghamton, New York native, Valeri Kathleen Paxton-Steele is the author of the paperback *Shadowstyx by Valkyri, Poetry and Prose of Depression* and the Kindle e-chapbook *Underneath: Poetry by Valeri Paxton-Steele*. Her writing primarily reflects her personal history of childhood sexual abuse, rape, domestic violence and mental illness. Her goal is to speak on behalf of victims and survivors of abuse. She contributed poems to the anthology *Silver Lining: Poets Against Violence* as well as a short story to the upcoming anthology *100 Voices, Volume II*.

Liz Priesendorf

Liz Priesendorf is a woman, wife, mother, and grandmother. A ten-year-old kid in a 45-year-old body, she enjoys reading, camping, canoeing, and anything outdoors with her family. Owned by four, loving dogs—Black, Roxie, Me-off, and Poncho—Liz is well-treated and her shots are kept up to date.

Linda Runnebaum

Linda Runnebaum, wife and mother of two teenage boys, has a day job at the Cooper County Memorial Hospital, but she hopes to write full time someday. She currently lives on a small farm in Boonville, Missouri, with her husband, sons, and lots of animals. When not writing, she enjoys reading anything she can get her hands on. She enjoys riding her Harley, gardening, cooking, baking, and hanging out with horses and other four-legged creatures. Her favorite authors are Stephen King and Janet Dailey. She writes about anything weird and unusual that comes into her mind.

Carole Kays Schaefer

Carole Kays Schaefer always held a desire to write. Upon retiring, she joined the Marshall Writers' Guild, where mentoring and advice helped her grow into a published author. Her writings have appeared in numerous newspapers and magazines. Her specialty is writing biography and preserving personal stories. She is an admirer of old-time story tellers, who used plot and a surprise ending. In 2005, she published *The John Jacob Feuers Family: 1803-2005*, a genealogy and collection of her maternal family's stories. Carole has edited Marshall Writers' Guild yearly anthologies since 2006. She is a member of the Missouri Writers' Guild.

Mary Silwance

Mary Silwance lives in Kansas City. An environmental activist, educator, farmhand, poet and mother, she is poetry co-editor for *Kansas City Voices* and member of the Kansas City Writers Group. Her work has appeared in *Konza Journal; Descansos; Heartland: Poems of Love, Resistance, and Solidarity; Sequestrum; Well Versed* and *Rock Springs Review*.

Irene Sims

Irene Thomas Sims has always lived in the Marshall area, graduated from Marshall High School, attended Missouri Valley College, graduated from CMSU at Warrensburg. She taught twenty-eight years in the Marshall Public Schools, retiring in 1992. She and her husband, Raymond Lee Sims, have lived on Wildcat Road since 1973. She and her husband are members of First Baptist Church and she serves on the Historical Committee. She is president of the Little Dixie Chapter of Missouri Animal Husbandry Association, member of Saline County Retired Teachers, and a member of Marshall Writers' Guild.

Billie Holladay Skelley

Billie Holladay Skelley is a registered nurse and an award-winning author. She received her bachelor's and master's degrees from the University of Wisconsin in Madison. She has written health related articles for both professional and lay journals. Her poems, articles, and essays have appeared in various journals, magazines, and anthologies in print and online. She has also written books for children.

Marilyn K. Smith

Marilyn K. Smith is an award-winning author, poet, photographer. Writing credits: *Buffalo Reflex Newspaper* (weekly column for thirty-plus years), *The Ozarks Mountaineer, Springfield! Magazine, Ozarks Watch magazine* (published through Missouri State University), *Springfield News-Leader* (guest columnist), *Ozark Senior Living* (associate editor), *Journal of the Ozarks* (contributing editor), and others. Poetry, fiction and nonfiction in 19 or more anthologies. Books: *Ozarks Recipes, Momma's, Mine and Others, and maybe a tale or two, A History of Highway 65, from the middle of the road, The Window Pane Inn, My Red Convertible, After a Hard Day on the Farm, Those were the Days on the Farm,* and *Bessie's Secret and other short stories.*

ে স

Notes on the Editor

Judy Stock is a white-haired, old rebel-rouser. She hasn't decided whether her husband supports her in her writing/editing/publishing endeavors, or if he just lets her spend her time involved in those things, so he can follow his own agenda.

She loves poetry and pairs up with another poet two times a year, during April, which is Poetry Month, and during November, which is the poet's answer to NaNoWriMo, to write a Poem-A-Day (PAD) and two on Tuesday. PAD can be accessed on the Poetic Asides blog on the Writer's Digest website.

She has received awards for her poetry from Writer's Digest, Ozarks Writers League, Missouri Writers' Guild, and more.

The rest of the time she does editing to help pay for her deep-down love of "hands-on" publishing.

She was on the Anthology committee for Columbia Chapter of Missouri Writers' Guild for seven issues of Well Versed, where she did most of the computer work, formatting and such, during that time, and assisted with editing the rest of it. She was managing editor of the 2010 edition, which received the Anthology of the Year Award from the Missouri Writers' Guild.

She is a member of Missouri Writers' Guild, where she has served on the President's Contest committee for several years, Ozarks Writers League, Marshall Chapter of Missouri Writers' Guild, and Boonslick Creative Writers.

Her published work includes *Does the Sun Have Fun?*, *Staging Whimsical Tea Parties*, and *Downward Spiral*. Her work was included in *Mysteries of the Ozarks, Vol. 4*; *Interpretations 1, 2, and 3*; the *Haiku Journal;* and Columbia Chapter of the Missouri Writers' Guild's *Well Versed* for several years. Judy also writes a weekly column for *The Boonslick Weekly*.

She is considering the reincarnation of the Rock Springs Review literary journal, and is also already thinking about another anthology.

For those of you not familiar with *Rock Springs Review,* please look at the next page and read what she wrote in the Summer 1998 issue, the first one she printed.

In case you were wondering?

There have been some changes made. Daren Dean, the founder, has retired from publishing the *Rock Springs Review.*

As a student in creative writing, Daren saw a need for a publication to serve the unestablished authors and poets in the area. He met this need by founding a small literary magazine that utilized submissions of short fiction, poetry, essays, interviews, and short articles.

The premiere issue was printed in Summer 1996.

Daren succeeded in placing an appropriate, upscale publication within reach of area authors, providing them with a writer-friendly venue. In addition, he succeeded in providing discriminating readers with some of the best work from heretofore unknown authors.

The time constraints of job and family, as well as continuing with his studies, led Daren to make the decision to step down as publisher.

I feel honored he has graciously allowed me to step in and continue with the *Rock Springs Review.* While I may make some minor changes, I hope to continue his lead in providing a quality publication for the readers and writers in the area.

Judy Stock